Genocide

P9-DEZ-986

Genocide

Ward Rutherford

BB

Editor-in-Chief: Barrie Pitt
Editor: David Mason
Art Director: Sarah Kingham
Picture Editor: Robert Hunt
Designer: David Allen
Cover: Denis Piper
Special Drawings: John Batchelor
Photographic Research: Carina Dvorak
Cartographer: Richard Natkiel

A new and perverted science

Introduction by Barrie Pitt

This is an account of the progression of German treatment of the Jews, from commonplace antisemitism which was part and parcel of the National Socialist Party dogma from its inception, to the ruthless application of what Hitler called the 'Final Solution'.

Germany, after the end of the First World War, provided a rich loam of frustration and discontent into which the seeds of racialism could be cast. Bolshevists and Jews were ready-made scapegoats for Germany's defeat and to attribute that failure to the machinations and subversive activities of these groups helped to make unpleasant reality more acceptable to many Germans. The National Socialist Party – itself a product of national reaction to bitter defeat and post-war economic chaos – issued in February 1924 a manifesto in which its racialist doctrines were stated in unequivocal language; German citizenship, it declared, should only be available to those of German blood, and it went on to state specifically that no Jew therefore could be a national. Even before the party manifesto had been published, Hitler had made public his own antisemitic feelings; *Mein Kampf*, written when he was imprisoned after the unsuccessful Munich 'putsch' of 1923, contained a crude indictment of the Jews for their part in undermining Germany's war effort.

With hatred of the Jews early established as an integral part of Nazi philosophy, it followed that those who were first to espouse the National Socialist cause should share the fanatical antisemitism of Hitler, for at this point in time the party was not so successful that it attracted adherents anxious only to climb on to its bandwagon. One of the 'first generation' Nazis, only too ready to absorb the outlandish theories of Nordic racial superiority, was Heinrich Himmler.

Commencing with an unpaid position within the Party, Himmler was eventually rewarded with a paid post and later was given the apparently nugatory appointment of second-in-command of the SS, a small inner group of Ernst Röhm's all-powerful SA. This somewhat insignificant section was to burgeon and flower like some sinister and evil plant, to choke its parent body almost to death and then throw out tendrils to gather to itself the instruments of power of the totalitarian state.

Hermann Göring actually created the infamous State Secret Police, or Gestapo, and inaugurated, in 1933, the concentration camps into which those unfortunates branded as enemies of the State were unceremoniously herded; but it was Himmler who was given eventual control of these organisations of terror and death. When Himmler created an SS Intelligence Department (SD), he appointed Reinhard Heydrich to its head, a young man of Nordic appearance and satisfactory physical strength, the very antithesis of the Reichsführer-SS himself. These two men complemented one another; the one concerning himself with concocting crackpot racialist theories, the other pursuing a source of personal power and self-aggrandisement. They were a formidable combination, and, well served by such men as Adolf Eichmann, they set about, with typical German efficiency, implementing the savage racial policies of the megalomaniac Führer.

Within weeks of Hitler coming to power in 1933, the Jewish incumbents of public office were being ruthlessly weeded out and Jewish professional and business men were being boycotted and harassed. From then onwards, persecution of Jews followed an inevitable progression; from harassment, through ridicule and vilification, exploitation and deportation, to the 'Final Solution' – total annihilation. As the numbers of Germany's conquests grew, so more and more Jews came within the grasp of Himmler's SS, and the graph of Jewish deaths showed a steady upwards climb.

To keep pace with the increasing flow of victims it was necessary to improve and make more efficient the methods of putting them to death. In the spring of 1942, the gas-chambers of Auschwitz-Birkenau began operating, each capable of applying the 'Final Solution' to 2,000 unfortunate people at a time. Gas was introduced into the chambers by dropping Zyklon B crystals into the ventilator shafts, and the bodies of the victims were later removed and destroyed in crematoria nearby. The whole ghastly and inhuman process was given an air of unreality by the playing of music from Lehar and Strauss during the grisly operation by an orchestra of potential victims.

The names of the concentration camps – Treblinka, Sobibor, Majdanek, Belsec, Chelmno, Dachau, Dora, Mauthausen, Ravensbrück, Sachsenhausen, and Buchenwald, have become grimly evocative, bringing to mind films taken by the Allies as these camps were overrun, recording for posterity the awful reality of what it meant to be a political prisoner of the Third Reich: skeletal figures clad in rags and barely distinguishable from their dead comrades; survivors almost too far gone to grasp that they had at last been 'liberated'.

These names are the battle honours of the SS 'Death's Head' units formed to provide staffs for the concentration camps, whose enemies were the men, women and children of the 'inferior' races, who had committed no crime but were condemned to death through an accident of birth.

Even with so many camps working feverishly to implement the Führer's orders, it was difficult to keep pace with the train-loads of unfortunates brought in from all over Europe; and so the victims were forced to suffer the final indignity of gross overcrowding in the death-chambers. Jammed together, hands raised above their heads and with small children thrown in on top, they were abused until their last moments on earth.

As the author points out, persecution of the Jews was no new thing. Throughout history the Jewish race has been vilified, segregated, discriminated against – often with the full support of the law – in countries the world over, and instances of Jews being the victims of bloody massacres are too frequent and too widespread. But the followers of Hitler brought another dimension into this persecution; where previously excesses against Jews had been perpetrated when passions ran high, Himmler, Heydrich and their like introduced an unemotional, inhuman and cold-blooded efficiency into the committing of genocide. The millions of Jews who died in the concentration camps of Nazi Germany were the victims of a new and perverted science.

The Nazis predecessors

There can surely be nothing which better justifies Gibbon's famous definition of history as 'little more than the register of the crimes, follies and misfortunes of mankind' than the treatment of the Jewish minorities. For almost 2,000 years Gentiles have shown their gratitude to those who gave them a unique vision of their relation with the Infinite, and who provided the milieu, intellectual and geographical, for the birth of Christianity, by persecutions which have changed over the centuries only in that they have grown in magnitude and ingenuity. As Bernard Levin wrote recently, reviewing a book on these two millenia, while most religions and peoples have been persecuted by someone at some time, 'only the Jews have always been persecuted by everybody'.

But if Christian and post-Christian civilisation has demonstrated a peculiar distinction in this respect, the race was already old in suffering long before the birth of Christ. They knew occupation of their nation-state almost from its inception; its people had experienced deportation and enforced exile under Assyrians, Egyptians and Babylonians. Attempts to compel them to desert the one god for the state pantheon were made by almost every one of these oppressors and later by both Greece and Rome. Endeavours in this direction by Antiochus III, the Seleucid, led to the successful rebellion of Judas Maccabeus in 167 BC.

When Tiberius became emperor in AD 14 his policy towards the Jewish members of the Roman Empire was like Hitler's 'extermination of the whole Jewish race'. The Romans were scandalised by the impudence of a tiny nation which could dare to consider its own religion superior to theirs.

In AD 30 the Sanhedrin, the Jewish High Court, lost jurisdiction over its own people. In AD 70, the Temple at Jerusalem was destroyed by Titus, after a Jewish revolt. In AD 132 there began the rebellion of Bar-Cochba which was ruthlessly suppressed by the Romans. This, the last revolt of the Jews against a foreign tormentor until the Warsaw ghetto rising of 1943, led the Romans to expel them from Jerusalem, destroying and ploughing up the city.

The expulsion of the Jews from Jerusalem is usually taken as the beginning of the period of Diaspora, or dispersal. In fact, under the goad of constant persecution at home, communities of Jews had already emigrated to other countries.

If, however, the Romans thought the Jewish nation and its insolent people had been suppressed, they were wrong. A year or two after the fall of their religious and governmental capital, a disaster of a kind which had preceded the total eclipse of other nations, the Jews rallied round their faith once more. A new centre was started at Jamnia on the Mediterranean coast, where new rabbinic schools were founded and the Sanhedrin re-established.

But these were small groups, and as the exiled people of a repressed nation, the Jews sought sanctuary wherever it could be found. They were

Heavily embroidered Thora from 1750

Above left: The Jewish inhabitants of
Cesarea suffer insults by the Greeks on
their Sabbath-day.
Left: Pilate persecutes the Jews.
Above: The Jews are expelled from
Jerusalem during the reign of Emperor
Hadrian

The synagogue in Berlin in 1864

usually welcome until Constantine made his own brand of Christianity the religion of the Roman Empire. When the empire divided, the Jews in western Europe lost all the privileges granted to them earlier. There was, at first, no intention to single them out; only to see that the important offices were filled by devotees of the new established faith. In the centuries that followed, however, persecution was to become so widespread, so diverse in form, that there is not one aspect of Nazi tyranny for which earlier exemplars cannot be found.

Separated more and more from their fellow men, the Jews became the canvas on which every human vice was portrayed. They were deicides (for had they not acceded in Christ's crucifixion?); they were the poisoners of wells; they were infanticides, re-enacting the crucifixion on baptised Christian children and using their blood for Passover Bread.

The church's view is adequately summed up in a series of eight sermons delivered by St John Chrysostom in 387. The Jews, he averred, were carnal, lascivious, avaricious; they were drunkards, whoremongers and criminals. His views and others like them found frequent echo down the centuries and from the mouths of Christian leaders. There are those who seek to explain antisemitism as an economic product—the jealous manifestation of those who have suffered from the competition caused by a diligent and gifted minority in their midst. History does not support the view. Persecution of the Jews was fomented from the top, by those who did not suffer from such competition. Ordinary working people in the Europe of the Middle Ages, as in Hitler's Germany, hated the persecutions and lost rather than benefited from them.

The sight of the Jews suffering, the Jews who had brought death to man's redeemer, was supposed to be edifying, in the same way that public executions were held to be edifying, as demonstrating the triumph of justice, divine and temporal, and as providing an awesome warning of the results of stubborn impenitence.

The pogroms and ghetto massacres promoted by the Crusaders of Hitler's New Order emulated earlier models, for each of the Crusades was preceded by massacres of 'the Saracens in our midst', the despoilers of the Holy Places, in France, Germany, Spain and England. When Benedict, leader of the Jewish community of York, came to London in 1189 to bring gifts for the coronation of Richard Coeur de Lion he was rewarded by being murdered, with scores of his fellows in the city. His death was followed by massacres in Norwich, Stamford and Kings Lynn, culminating in one in York itself. Here a group of Jews finally chose suicide in preference to the violence of the mob.

Just as the citizenship laws of the Nazis made Jews second class citizens without rights, so in medieval England they were the property of the king. As their synagogues were burned in Germany, so they had been

Above : Fugitive Jews pitch camp at Gibraltar during their flight from Morocco.
Below : Jews of Cologne are burned alive

burned in Rome and Spain. As the Nazis extorted money from the Jews, so earlier had kings and prelates in Christian Europe. The great churches and cathedrals which stand as the pride of Christendom were largely built from such funds, often extracted under torture and with the torturers receiving ecclesiastical and even papal blessing. As the Nazis forced emigration and expulsion of the Jews so had they been expelled from England and France.

The theories of Jewish conspiracies had their beginnings in the Middle Ages. In Spain the clergy preached the need for the country to rid itself of the Jews. Jews, they said, planned the enslavement of all Spaniards from the King downwards. Thousands died in the massacres thus inspired.

The Middle Ages, too, saw the start of the ghetto system in which Jew was segrated from Aryan, a system which was to be used so efficiently in Poland and Russia in the 1940s. Bitter as the insult was, it gave to the Jews thus enclosed some measure of security, and the Jews returned to the inbred and introspective comforts of the ghetto whenever danger threatened.

As the Germans instituted a bureaucracy of organised murder, so too did Torquemada, the first Grand Inquisitor, a worthy predecessor of Heydrich and Eichmann.

As Himmler preached on the transcendant virtue of purity of blood, so in 17th Century Spain 'limpieza de sangre' was the excuse for turning upon the Jewish polluters. As the Nazis rewrote history to exhibit Jewish guilt so in the Middle Ages the masses were taught that the Jews were the tribe of Judas Iscariot, the Christ-betrayer.

When existence in western Europe became intolerable the Jews began to move eastwards. Here, they were told, more reasonable attitudes prevailed. And so at first it proved. In Austria their rights as human beings and full citizens were confirmed.

In Poland, Hungary, Rumania, at the level of ordinary humanity, Jew and Christian lived happily together. But the Church was uneasy at such an alliance.

An opportunity occurred for suppression of the Jews when war broke out between the Russians and Poles. In Poland they were said to be in league with Russia; in Russia, in league with the Poles. Thousands were put to death.

As the Jews, according to witnesses, faced the Nazi shootings without a plea for mercy, so they went to the stake, singing psalms and refusing the recantation and conversion which could save them. Among the individual stories of these mass-burnings which have reached us is that of a small boy who encouraged and consoled his younger brother as he recoiled from the flames into which he was about to be thrown, by telling him he would go to Paradise. So later, fathers, mothers, grandparents and elder brothers and sisters were to console terrified younger ones in the death pits of Ponary and the gas-chambers of Auschwitz.

Even with The Enlightenment there came no relief. Science was distorted in order to justify persecution and reason was held in abeyance. Voltaire himself could break the flow of his logic to assail the Jews as ignorant, barbarous, avaricious, superstitious, filled with hatred.

In Russia the pogrom had become an instrument of government policy to be applied whenever the people became restive. Even in the 1914 war with Germany, persecution of the Jews was granted no moratorium. It was still being fanned when, as happened in Germany later, it threatened the conduct of the war.

And it was from Tsar Nicholas's own press, at his country residence, Tsarskoye Selo, that in 1905 – the year of unsuccessful revolution – the

A traditional Jewish wedding during the early 1800s

14

A political cartoon from the late 1800s depicts the exodus of Jews from Germany

Richard Wagner

Stewart Houston-Chamberlain

notorious 'Protocols of the Elders of Zion' was issued. This product of some paid government hack was an amalgam of all the absurd myths of Jewish international plots from the Middle Ages, and it was still being called in evidence by Hitler thirty years later. Tsar Nicholas II was not, however, a man to whom reason was ever of much significance when it came to attacking the Jews: he had told Kaiser Wilhelm II of Germany about the English: 'The Englishman is a *Yid*'.

In the rest of Europe the populist and democratising movements of the mid-19th Century produced a new stick with which to beat the Jews and were responsible for introducing the word 'antisemitism' into language. If you were an opponent of democratic movements and an antisemite, like Gobineau, the Jews were communists and socialists. If you were a socialist and an antisemite, like Drumont, then the Jews were the financial *éminences noires* of capitalism.

Joseph Arthur, Count Gobineau, (1816-82) sought in his four volume *Essai sur l'Inégalité des Races Humaines* to explain history in racial terms. It was, he claimed, an eternal conflict between the dolichocephalic (or long-headed) races and the brachycephalic (or broad-headed) races. Foremost among the dolichocephalics were the blond Nordic peoples. The Jews, of course, were brachycephalics. So pervasive were his ideas that British propagandists looking for a new pejorative to apply to the Germans called them 'brachycephalics'.

Edouard Drumont (1844-1917) merged antisemitism not only with socialism, but with the occult as well – a combination also to be found among the Nazis. And it was one of his followers, Jacques de Biez, who coined the name 'National Socialists'. He said in 1889: 'We are socialists. We are national socialists, because we are attacking international finance. We want France for the French.' With 'Germany' and 'the Germans' substituted in that

18

last sentence, the passage could have come from Goebbels.

The persecutions that took place in Russia, Poland, Rumania and Hungary drove the Jews westward once more. Many got no further than Austria, but smaller numbers reached Germany, France and beyond. They were accepted, but welcomed by none. Bred in the ghettoes, their natural instinct was to cling together, holding on to their habits, customs and language, ever fearful of new pogroms.

The church saw them once more as a threat to the faith of its flock. Judaism, they contended, was the antithesis of Christianity. Furthermore, since history had shown the Jews to be unconvertible they must be ejected. Even baptised Jews were probably fraudulent 'spies-within-the-Church' and for the good of Christianity must be treated like their unbaptised fellows. The mercantile and trading classes saw them as competition. The assimilated middle class Jews of Vienna and Berlin viewed them with frank disgust, as poor relations who had suddenly descended on the family home. They were chagrined to find, in addition, that gentiles refused to accept their protests that they came uninvited. 'This', the gentiles told one another, 'is what happens when you let a Jew in. Before you know where you are he has brought his whole family.'

There were other factors at work in Germany. The Franco-Prussian War of 1870 had been followed by an economic crisis, while the movement towards the unification of the German states into one nation, started by Bismarck, was still progressing. Inevitably, this focused attention upon race, upon 'German-ness'.

The emigrés from the east with their strange customs and dress did not conform with this racial image. In a community of states suddenly conscious of itself as one people there was no place for the sad-eyed men with their long black overcoats, beards, curled temple locks and flat hats. 'The Jews,' one 19th Century writer stated 'are our bad luck.' His phrase was to become a Nazi slogan.

But it was felt that if life were made uncomfortable enough for them they might get up and go away, and the antisemitic movements directed their efforts towards this end. There was already a substantial body of antisemitic literature, and as more appeared the views expressed became increasingly passionate. At first the Jews were 'aliens' or 'decadent', as they became again in Nazi language of 1933-35; before the end of the century they were 'parasites' and 'vermin', fit only 'to be trodden underfoot'.

Darwin's theory of evolution, which first upset the pet delusions of humanity in the 1850s, was rapidly applied to the social scene by interpreters who made up in dogmatism what they lacked in understanding. Evolution, in their view, imparted a scientific credibility to antisemitism. These misconceptions also were to be taken up by Nazism which called itself 'the biological will of the people'.

Thousands of doors hitherto open to the Jews in Germany and Austria were abruptly slammed. The university societies adopted resolutions banning Jews from membership. The elite regiments and the army officer reserve would no longer accept them. Clubs, societies, and chambers of trade had tacit agreements that Jews were not to be admitted.

Frenchmen and Germans, otherwise enemies, found a common cause here, For it was to French thought on the subject that the Germans turned. There was, for example, a Gobineau Society in Freiburg. But the French, a nation of intellectual speculators, have rarely acted upon the products of their speculations. With the Germans it was otherwise. Even the most outrageous philosophy was something to be lived out.

Gobineau had been a personal friend of Richard Wagner the composer, who had already attacked the

A cruel version of the German
national arms: an illustration of the
anti-Jewish feeling which grew as a
result of the Treaty of Versailles

Eure jetzigen Führer!

Wollt Ihr Andere?

Dann wählt deutschnational!

'Your present leaders. Do you want
others? Then vote Deutschnational.'

memory of the dead Mendelssohn, on the grounds that he was a Jew, from whom he had received nothing but kindness and encouragement. To the composer of 'Tannhäuser' and 'The Ring' Mendelssohn's music now appeared 'strange, cold, bizarre, mediocre, unnatural and perverse'. It was Wagner's antisemitism which, assuredly, commended him to Hitler as much as his music.

The Wagner home provided a gathering place for 'intellectual' antisemitism. Hitler was to be a visitor there. But an earlier one had been Stewart Houston-Chamberlain (1855-1927), the British antisemite and First World War German propagan-

dist. Chamberlain was Wagner's biographer and married his daughter. It is to him that we are indebted for the first logically consistent assertion of the antisemite's position: 'I hate the Jews. I hate their star and their cross'.

The outcome of the First World War brought a new impetus to antisemitism. Defeat was a deeply traumatic experience for the Germans and the Austrians. During the last week in October 1918 the German army was advancing. By the next week, on 7th November, an armistice was being arranged. As a result the Germans were to find themselves at the mercy of the Entente Powers

German troops return to Berlin, 1918

who had never ceased to regard Germany, even after a change to liberal government, as an aggressive militarist. Their fury was the greater because they had never really broken the fighting will of that aggressor at the front. Thousands of soldiers, undefeated, tramped back to Germany, to find a country economically broken and unable to support them. Something, they reasoned, must have happened beyond the obvious, beyond the mutiny at Kiel and the stringencies of the British blockade, to bring this about.

It was certain, after all the centuries of vilification and oppression and the unremitting build up of antisemitism as an intellectual force, that sooner or later there would be an eruption. It was thus that the Jews came to be held responsible for Germany's 'stab in the back'. The Jews, who found friends among the new liberal government, and were in that government itself, were held to form part of the great conspiracy aimed at Germany's overthrow; and antisemitism, at best the idiosyncratic *idée fixe* of certain individuals or groups, was now a powerful force. Like a new religion it set out on a career of proselytisation.

The years of harassment

Hitler was, of course, an antisemite from the beginning. From the time, that is to say, of his earliest recorded utterances. His much-quoted sentence in *Mein Kampf* which states that had 12,000 to 15,000 'of these Hebrew enemies' been gassed at the beginning of and during the First World War 'the sacrifices of millions at the front would not have been in vain' was probably written in 1923, when he was in Landsberg Prison, but he had expressed similar sentiments in a speech in 1920 and in a letter in 1919.

His ideas on the subject were probably formed mainly during his struggling days in Vienna – a time when he was not too proud to accept the money sent to him by a Jewish friend of the family. His associates, the embittered frequenters of the doss-houses – antiMarxists, antisemites and panGermanists – killed time, their only freely available commodity, in the vain search for scapegoats for Germany's woes which they believed were the cause of their own.

Historians seeking a philosophical base for Hitler's antisemitism have suggested a number of sources, among others the notions of the Cistercian monk, Adolf Lenz. His views, propagated in the *Aribheröiken*, largely correspond with Hitler's. He too supported the theory of Aryan 'superiority' and advocated the elimination of the Jews by sterilisation and deportation. But the truth is such searches for inspiration are futile; Hitler's antisemitism never had an intellectual base and, in private, he poured scorn on the pan-German racial theories of Alfred Rosenberg and Walter Darré. In so far as he had to justify his stand, from time to time, his arguments were drawn at random out of concepts from Gobineau, Nietzsche with his *Ubermensch*, Darwin (Hitler was forever talking about the 'survival of the

Prayers for the harassed Jews of Germany in a New York synagogue

fittest' and 'natural selection') and, in particularly, the '*salon* antisemitism' of the Wagners and Stewart Houston-Chamberlain.

Hitler's antisemitism, like all true racialism, was emotional and subjective. When one begins analysing psychological motives the difficult area of sexual inadequacy and frustration has to be considered. For just as white racialists of today talk of the supposed lusts and gross penises of Negroes, so Hitler wrote of Jewish youths lying lasciviously in wait for German girls to drag them off and seduce them. In the half-world of his own fantasies these images could drive him to paroxysms of fury. There is no reason to believe him impotent or, as wartime gossip suggested, sexually-malformed. The Russian autopsy evidence shows that this was not so. But there is good reason to suppose that he was unattractive to girls, particularly in the days when he was poor. Apart from his dire poverty – for him undoubtedly a particular degradation – there was his gaucheness, his tendency to unprovoked fury, his burning-eyed fanaticism. And it is no coincidence that he so constantly reverts to the theme of Jewish finance as corrupting, for money is frequently an unconscious symbol for blood, and 'corrupting' the blood of Aryan girls was precisely what he saw his nightmare Jewish youths doing.

In the *Nationalsozialistische Deutsche Arbeiter-Partei*, to give the Nazis their full and proper title, his antisemitism was quickly given political embodiment. Points 4 and 5 of the NSDAP's manifesto, published in February 1924, stated that German citizenship was available to 'only those of German blood, regardless of religious persuasion'. In case the meaning of that sentence should be ambiguous: 'No Jew', it declares, 'can, therefore, be a national'. This is developed in the succeeding point which states that those who do not possess state citizen-

Ernst Röhm

ship are subject 'to the laws applying to aliens'.

These principles were incorporated not merely into the party's ideology, but also into its behaviour. Always para-military in character (it claimed to be fighting a battle against the Communists), the party militia was Captain Ernst Röhm's *Sturmabteilung* (Storm Detachments or, more popularly, Storm Troopers). When not parading and tilting at the windmills of Bolshevism they were intimidating Jews or provoking intimidations by inflammatory speeches on street corners.

Already, however, a new group was growing up within the militia itself. In 1922 a special unit of the SA had been formed and given the name *Schutzstaffeln* (Protection Formations) or, for short, SS. Three years later a puny, myopic Bavarian with a receding blue chin, a man who had few other qualities than a plodding

and conscientious execution of party duties, and whose name was Heinrich Himmler, joined the NSDAP. In 1926, with the SS then numbering 200 men and mainly responsible for stewarding party meetings, he was made second in command. In 1929, at the direct order of Hitler, Himmler, then twenty-eight, was appointed to succeed Erhard Heiden as commander, or *Reichsführer*, of the SS. The body had grown by eight men, but was still subservient to the SA and Röhm.

If Himmler gave an impression of small imagination, he enjoyed, like Hitler, a strong fantasy-life peopled by the characters of Germanic legend. Through the SS he saw how such dreams might be realised. It was to become a powerful, independent force in Nazism and in Germany, a state within the state. Its members were to be something between a new order of Teutonic Knights and a Society of Jesus in the party – for his dreams

Heinrich Himmler

Police keep a watchful eye on
marching SA

SS parade

Reinhard Heydrich

SA storm troops make an arrest outside their Berlin HQ

SA troops advocate a boycott of Jewish goods

Below: Desecration of a Jewish cemetery

A poster announces an early
Goebbels speech; his theme:
'Prepare to leave for Palestine'

always bore a tinge of mysticism.

Uniformed in black, highly disciplined in contrast to the unruly SA, the SS quickly attracted members in such numbers that of those who reached the qualifying requirements (would-be recruits had to prove the purity of their Nordic blood back to 1750) only one in ten could be accepted. By the time of the invasion of Poland the SS numbered 26,000.

In June 1931 a blond, blue-eyed young man from Waldtrudering, who had recently joined the SS, was introduced to Himmler through the good offices of one of his own staff. He was Reinhard Heydrich, who had been won for Nazism by his fiancée, Lina von Osten, when he had been forced to resign his commission in the navy after a scandal involving a shipyard director's daughter.

Himmler had, at the time, plans for an Intelligence service of his own in the SS, although one of his party associates, Hermann Göring, had always appeared to regard police and security as his province. Himmler's effort was, therefore, bound to be in competition, but he was always a master schemer. He appointed the young Heydrich to head this new department, to which the name of *Sicherheitsdienst* (SD) or security service, was given. It had power to watch over and keep files on even the highest party members. Thus were brought into collusion the two men who between them and from very different traits of character were to take such a toll of human life. Himmler was a man convinced by cranky theories of 'blood and soil' which fate had put him in the position of implementing. He was not a sadist. He took no pleasure in the suffering he was to impose. On the contrary,

A British cartoon attacks German anti-semitism

ALL FOOLS' DAY IN GERMANY.

CHANCELLOR HITLER: "AS A RETALIATION FOR THE FALSE STATEMENT BY FOREIGNERS THAT WE **HAVE** BEEN PERSECUTING THE JEWS, I FORBID YOU TO ENTER THIS SHOP."

Left: Hermann Göring. *Above and Below:* Dachau in 1933

like an Inquisitor, he deplored its necessity. The only time he witnessed an execution, at Minsk in 1941, he was afflicted with hysteria, drew the reproof of the firing squad commander, and fainted. Yet he gave the orders which sent millions to their death.

There is no sign that Heydrich either was in the strict sense a sadistic or blood-thirsty man, and unlike Himmler, he was not a devotee of any theory. Indeed he would probably, in secret, have ridiculed such things. He was, however, a man of heady ambition and shared and surpassed his master's gift for intriguing. He was, in the widest and most literal meaning of that word, an amoral man, who simply saw where advantage lay and knew how to take it. Other Nazis at least claimed to have had some kind of internal conflict before bringing themselves to do what was asked of them. Heydrich never once showed any sign that he was troubled. Had the Nazi Party been founded on the concept that the presence of Jews in Germany was its greatest fortune and that they should be rewarded for their mere existence Heydrich might well have carried out the duties involved with the same zeal, especially as he himself had some Jewish blood.

Himmler, who suffered terrible conflicts (which probably caused his stomach-cramps of the later war years), overcame them through his belief that 'purity of blood' was so all-important that it expunged every other scruple, including loyalty to his chief, Ernst Röhm. For in the summer of 1934, a year-and-a-half after Hindenburg had appointed Hitler Chancellor, Himmler made himself party to a plot among those Nazis who feared the SA as a private army. This led to the murder of Röhm and hundreds of his subordinates. The excuse was that Röhm was planning a

Oranienburg

Adolf Eichmann

coup or Putsch against Hitler, and the success with which the Röhm group was destroyed left Himmler's SS in virtual control of the field. The SA had gained Germany a great deal of international notoriety by its overt and unbridled brutality towards the Jews – particularly now that the Communists had been pushed into hiding. The SS were plainly more disciplined, more formal in procedure, in a word, more gentlemanly. Nonetheless, many people realised that in Himmler and Heydrich they had a couple more devious and, in the long term, more dangerous than the candidly savage Röhm.

While these convulsions were taking place either unknown or with no significance attached to them by the majority of the German people, the NSDAP now in power was spreading the flames of antisemitism throughout the land. The party manifesto, written nearly ten years earlier, had laid down that Jews were to be treated as aliens. Aliens can always be asked by their host country to 'go home'. But the Jews of Germany, unlike other aliens, had no home; furthermore, many of them had lived in the country for generations. Germany came before Judaism

Anti-Jewish rally in Berlin

for them. The policy, at first pursued more or less hapazardly, but later more purposefully and officially, was to make conditions in Germany so unbearable that many of these 'aliens' would choose to leave. But departure on those terms was possible only for the rich and influential who had the contacts which would make them welcome elsewhere. So if Hitler's policy did anything it coerced into leaving Germany the very people he most feared and (if his arguments were followed) would force them to become a cohesive group among Germany's enemies.

Nevertheless, as early as the spring of 1933, within weeks of Hitler's accession to power, Jews were being 'weeded out' of all public offices: Jewish lawyers, doctors, shopowners saw their business and practices boycotted. Those who refused to be intimidated were photographed and had their pictures published in local newspapers. Yet, as the American consul in Leipzig pointed out, the boycott was disliked by the public. The poorer people found themselves forced to use the Nazi-approved shops which were quick to raise their prices as competition was reduced; others detested the whole principle of such persecution. Outside Germany, as awareness grew of what was happening there, there was already revulsion which was having repercussions on diplomatic and trade relations.

Any group less maniacally obsessed with racialism might have seen that the time had come to abandon their antisemitic policies, but the Nazis even turned foreign criticism to their own ends by saying that their policy of persecution was in reprisal for atrocities and menaces by Jews abroad.

When a visiting South African Minister suggested that Hitler should find a solution to the Jewish problem in ways which did not antagonise Britain, the Führer launched into one of his diatribes of antisemitism which included the threat that 'one day the Jews would disappear from Europe'. To the Czechoslovakian Foreign Minister Hitler was even less equivocal: 'We are going to destroy the Jews . . . The day of reckoning has come'.

In the face of criticism, however, antisemitic measures had to be cloaked in law. Many people in Germany, as in other countries, believed the Jews to wield an influence and to hold an authority disproportionate to their numbers. Pressures on the Jewish community, by means of restrictive laws, were seen therefore as simply correcting this imbalance, and so they were made to appear unexceptionable. Their total effect was to divide Jew from Gentile; to make the existence of the Jew harsher, and by these joint effects to bring about both the means and excuse for total segregation of the minority community.

Had the Jews been guilty of all that was imputed to them, had the genetic theories borne the imprimatur of reputable science, this unleashing of the most contemptible elements in the community, this chivvying and bullying, would still have been inadmissable. It was only slightly less repellent perhaps than the acts of those who later took such a prominent role, none of whom had even the excuse that they were victims of the psychosis of racialism. On the one side there were the compulsive bullies and sadists to whom the identity of those at their mercy was indifferent; on the other, the conscientious and ambitious administrators who in their anxiety to impress superiors purposely extirpated from their souls the last shreds of decency.

The reality was that the Nazi case for the persecution of the Jews had few pretensions to intellectual seriousness. It was simply the way of satisfying that need for 'enemies' which at once justifies and excuses the inefficiency and oppressions of tyrants.

The oppressive nature of the régime was quickly made obvious to all Germans, gentile and Jew. It was obvious by, among other manifestations, the fact that so many of the Nazi leadership, once in the saddle, accreted to themselves police powers. Immediately after Hitler's ascent to the Chancellorship it was Göring, not Himmler, who opened the first concentration camps for political enemies. Less than a month after Hitler's appointment, on 28th February 1933, the day after the Reichstag fire, the first measure allowing the arrest of ordinary citizens and their condemnation to 'protective custody' for an indefinite period and with no appeal was agreed. Implementation of that decree was also undertaken by Göring. By April in Prussia alone, over 16,000 persons had been deprived of their liberty. By Christmas 1933 the numbers had grown to such proportions that Hitler was forced to announce an amnesty for 27,000 prisoners: there was no more room for them.

The camps in which they were incarcerated rapidly became places of ill-repute, whose keepers were responsible to no one. Himmler now began his own essays in this sphere, having already challenged Göring with his SD, and opened a 'model' concentration camp at Dachau, twelve miles from Munich. Here the Himmlerian ideals of order and discipline were put into practice. Characteristically, all camp existence was governed by a code of regulations which covered every eventuality from how floggings and hangings were to be carried out to how much the prisoner-hangman was to be paid for his services (three cigarettes!). Obscenely as these regulations now read, particularly when one realises that they related to men and women against whom no charge had ever been laid, they were, in contrast to the regulations at Göring's camps, intended to ensure an orderly administration.

For the men who would perform the duties of guards at Dachau and at future camps, a duty which he never ceased to regard as responsible, exacting and even painful in the extreme, Himmler opened yet another department of the SS, the *Totenköpf Verbände* or Death's Head units. Among those who joined the Dachau staff in this way was a young man called Adolf Eichmann, destined to rise so meteorically in the SS hierarchy.

Thus, by the end of 1934 Himmler had assured for himself a place almost unassailable, except by Hitler himself, in the new state. His Protection Formations contained their own secret service to hunt out the enemies of the state and to select places to which those enemies could be sent and kept. Himmler was on the way to making himself what he ultimately became, the second most powerful man in the Third Reich.

In 1934 as in 1933 there was no reduction in the tormenting of the Jews and every type of harassment was practised. Local authorities went far beyond their own legitimate rights and even flouted the German constitution. Jews were forbidden the parks, buses, and swimming pools, and in some places local government employees were required to sign a declaration that they had broken off social relations with any Jews they knew. The Nazis sometimes stopped these practices, knowing the effect they would have abroad, and it was part of their applied cunning that in so far as harassment was enshrined in statute or decree it was always justifiable by the Nazis on grounds of 'expediency'. Thus, when entry for Jews to German schools and colleges began to be calculated on their numbers in the population as a whole, the excuse was that it was 'to prevent overcrowding' in German institutions of learning.

In 1935 the first of Nuremberg Laws on Reich Citizenship which implemented the party's stated policy of turning Jews into aliens was announced by Hitler at one of the Nuremberg rallies on 15th September. Moderates in the party (of which there were many, though their voices and influence were always muted) accepted the laws on the understanding that they were an enactment made once for all time – actually they were extended by some thirteen supplementary decrees. Some even welcomed them as regularising the existing situation and by so doing at once showing the Jews where they stood and giving them a measure of protection under law, even if only as aliens, which in the previous state of affairs they had lacked. The truth was that such legalised social isolation of the Jews as came about through the laws did not merely make subsequent and harsher measures easier both juridically and psychologically, it was the essential prerequisite for them. The decrees made acceptable to the public the idea of two classes of citizen: *Reichsbürger*, who had to be of pure German blood, and *Staatsangehöriger* who though subjects were not entitled to citizenship. Such a division of men had not existed in law since the Roman Empire.

The first Nuremberg Laws proscribed the Jews from many activities including the Civil Service. They forbade intermarriage with Aryans, and more than this, the measures made the definition of a Jew broader than it had ever been in the minds of the Jew-baiting rabble rousers. As a consequence, people who were practising members of the Christian or other faiths could find to their horror that instead of being the 'good Germans' they had imagined themselves to be, they were labelled Jews and second class citizens. It was, however, notable that the Nuremberg Laws, neither in 1935 nor subsequently, attempted to define Jews. They were always described vaguely as 'aliens'. Even as late as

Mackensen, Hitler and Frick at the
Olympic Games in Berlin

Sigmund Freud

Max Planck

Albert Einstein

Herschel Grünspan

Count von Welczek, German Ambassador in Paris

Ernst vom Rath, third secretary at the embassy

the summer of 1943, Himmler forbade the publication of a decree which would define Jewishness. 'Such dogmatism ties our hands', he pointed out.

Immediate world reaction to the Nuremberg Laws was strongly critical. Berlin had been chosen as the venue for the 1936 Olympic Games but representation was made to the International Committee to change this, on the grounds that German government policy was sharply in contradiction to the spirit of the games. Hitler had set his heart on the Berlin Olympiad and the Nuremberg Laws were played down. The games took place and became a classic in Olympic annals. Once finished, the stream of antisemitic legislation followed steadily and unpityingly, eroding the position of the Jewish community. Jewish firms had to distinguish themselves and register. Individual Jews were expelled from the liberal professions and the universities, and in many cases forced to emigrate. So there began that exodus of men and women, of whom many, like Freud, Einstein and Max Planck, were world renowned figures.

The steady intensification of the Nuremberg measures was not enough in the Nazi view. Hitler was preoccupied with the polluting effect of Jewish finance on the Aryan economy. The Jews must, therefore, be forced outside it. But to do this far-reaching laws were needed and these had to be justified not only to German public opinion, but also to world opinion.

The next act in the drama of Nazi-relations was provoked by an incident outside Germany. On 7th November 1938 a seventeen-year-old German Jew, Herschel Grünspan, visiting an uncle in Paris, presented himself at the German Embassy there and asked to see the ambassador, Graf Johannes von Welczek. A third secretary, Ernst vom Rath – an official more august than a stranger calling unheralded at a major embassy had a right to expect – came to ask what he

Josef Goebbels

wanted. Grünspan drew a gun and shot him, claiming later that he took this young official for the ambassador. There were a number of suspicious circumstances surrounding the assassination: firstly, the absurd suggestion supposedly made by the killer that one so youthful could be the ambassador; secondly, the implied assumption that international envoys attended callers on their own doorsteps; and thirdly, the fact that vom Rath was an anti-Nazi already under Gestapo surveillance. Furthermore in Germany there was every sign that the outburst of violence which followed this event had been prepared well in advance, not least because those who might be accused of inciting it had taken the trouble to provide themselves with alibis.

The *Volkischer Beobachter* (People's Observer) which, under the slogan *Ein Volk, Ein Reich, Ein Führer*, purveyed the official party line, carried a leader on the killing on 7th November, the day it occurred. 'Obviously', it said, 'the German people will be able to draw their own conclusions about this new outrage.' On the night of 9th November Hitler went to a dinner in Munich in celebration of the 1923 Bierhalle plot and it was here that Josef Goebbels, Reich Minister of Propaganda and no. doubt part-inspirer if not author of that leader in *Volkischer Beobachter*, revealed that reprisals – by which he meant riots – were already going on.

After Goebbels's speech there was little doubt in the minds of the assembly that party leaders of all levels were expected to organise and oversee the implementation of riots, at the same time being careful not to be identified as their instigators. In this therefore they were following the example of their leaders, who were at the Munich dinner and could not be said to be connected with the violence. The only person who did not have this alibi was Göring, but he had made sure he was on a train bound for Berlin, while the one man who alone would have been able to provide the 'reprisal personnel', Reinhard Heydrich, was in Nuremberg. But there exists a teleprinter message sent by him that day, which instructs police chiefs in their duties in the riots likely to break out. These included making sure that no Aryan property was damaged, preventing the looting of shops and flats, while permitting their destruction, and making sure that no synagogue was fired if it was situated where the conflagration could endanger adjacent property. A further message circulated by one of his assistants ordered the state police to arrest between 20,000 and 30,000 Jews, particularly wealthy ones, and to seize synagogue archives.

During that night a tornado of fury fell upon the Jews of every major German city. Street gangs, unhampered by the police, looted and smashed 7,500 shops, set fire to at least 171 apartment houses and to almost 200 synagogues, including that of Nuremberg, the city in which Heydrich was staying. He feigned surprise at the news.

The rioters suffered only 117 arrests, but thirty-six Jews died (later this figure was raised to ninety-one), and another thirty-six were injured; 20,000 were taken into custody 'for their own protection'. Thus, the 'spontaneous wrath' of the German people over the killing of an unknown diplomat in Paris, turned not upon French residents of the country, but upon the Jews.

Of the detained Jews some 10,000 were sent to Buchenwald concentration camp, whence, in fact, many were ransomed.

Grünspan, if not himself the stooge of the Gestapo, was possibly egged on by their *agents provocateurs*, for what came to be called the *Kristallnacht* (mistranslated as 'The Night of Broken Glass'). In fact the riots

A Berlin synagogue is destroyed by fire

persisted for over a week and provided the excuse for new action against the German Jews of which advantage was swiftly taken.

Of Hitler's role in the *Kristallnacht* little is sure. His reaction to it was, in any case, typical of that hatred which paralysed his reasoning processes, for he at once and unconditionally accepted Jewish responsibility for it and issued a *diktat* to Göring. This instructed him to see that the Jewish question was 'coordinated and solved, once and for all'.

On 12th November, three days from the start of the riots, with the mobs still roaming the streets, Göring called a meeting at his Ministry of Aviation to consider Hitler's instructions. The deliberations of the Nazi chiefs were interrupted by a matter resulting from the riots; it now appeared that while the shops were certainly owned by Jews, the freeholds belonged in many cases to gentiles, some of whom had had millions of marks worth of damage done to their property, in particular through the smashing of plate glass

'The Night of Broken Glass'

windows, and were now claiming
from insurance companies. If the
companies paid up they would be
bankrupted. If they did not there
would follow a damaging loss of
confidence in German insurance. The
compromise reached by the meeting
was for a community fine on the Jews
which would pay for the damage – a
nice insight into National Socialist
attitudes – and the insurance companies' representative present at
the meeting was told by Göring to
see that fewer windows were broken
in future.

In due course the minutes of this
meeting were circulated. They laid
down the pattern for persecution as
it was to be repeated wherever the
Nazi writ ran. The Jews were to be
dispossessed of their property; state-
nominated trustees would take over
all their enterprises, paying them
derisory compensation. Over the next
weeks and months recommendations

from a select committee appointed
by the meeting were put into force.
Jews were prohibited from attending
German schools and from going to
cinemas and theatres. Plans were to
be laid down for the conscription of
Jews into forced labour gangs and a
tenancy law was drafted which allowed Jewish-owned property to be let
only to Jews – the basis of a ghetto
system. Whatever other evidence
there was, the speed with which these
measures were introduced after the
Paris incident was itself indicative of
of the fact that the forces of antisemitism were prepared.

If there was ever any doubt as to
the fate awaiting the German Jews,
Göring's meeting had dispelled it.
Announcing the thousand million
mark community fine to pay for the
damage, he said: 'If in the near future
the German Reich should come into
conflict with foreign Powers, it goes
without saying that we in Germany
would first of all let it come to a
reckoning with the Jews.'

An article in the SS journal *Das Schwarze Korps* on 24th November – a fortnight after the meeting in Göring's office – was still less equivocal. Any Jews left in Germany after an outbreak of war would, the writer declared, be 'annihilated'.

Important as such racial and ideological questions might be, Heydrich, Göring and their colleagues saw that in the short run there were economic advantages to be gained by using the Jews for a kind of sustained international blackmail. Heydrich had already been 'permitting' Jewish emigration in return for payments in foreign currency which Germany needed and, since the *Kristallnacht,* he had 20,000 Jews in custody and purposely subjected to such conditions in Buchenwald that they could be expected to be ready to pay even the most extortionate sums for their freedom.

But Germany's attempts to solve its so-called 'Jewish problem' were not confined to internal efforts. It had, in common with Poland and Rumania, persuaded the world that its desire to rid itself of part of its own population was a problem others could help to solve. To this end, on the initiative of President Roosevelt, a conference of thirty-two nations had taken place at Evian, in Switzerland, in the July of 1938, where the question of what was to be done with the unwanted Jews of these three countries was discussed – without result. The conference broke up with no one willing to take even Jewish children. For Hitler and his fellow-antisemites the failure of the conference, though it still left them saddled with their own 'Jewish problem', was evidence that the world was largely apathetic towards the fate of the Jews. Whatever the Germans now did to the Jews they were doing largely as a favour to the rest of the world, which by its apathy at the conference, had accepted implicit responsibility for the fate of the German Jews. The *Kristallnacht*

had been one quick result of this failure.

A variety of schemes were toyed with, all aimed at ridding Germany of its Jewish population in ways which would avoid too direct an affront to world opinion. A plan which the German Minister of Economics, Hjalmar Schacht, put for using Jewish assets to fund a loan to be used to assist 'orderly Jewish emigration' and which was taken as far as London for discussion in the December of 1938, collapsed when Hitler quarrelled with Schacht. Another scheme was the famous Madagascar Project by which the German Jews were to be accommodated in a 'reserve' in this French colony. The idea is said to have originated from the French Foreign Minister, who said that his own government were thinking of sending 10,000 Jews there. None of these proposals ever materialised.

Europe was now moving towards the situation the German Jews, who since Evian knew themselves without friends, dreaded most – war between Germany and the major powers. At the same time the number of Jews in German hands was growing with the accession of new territories. The *Anschluss* in Austria had brought 185,000 under Nazi domination and exactly the same pattern of harassment was applied here as in the Reich. Its result – a satisfactory one to the young Lieutenant Adolf Eichmann, who had been put in charge of emigration in Vienna – was the departure of 45,000 Austrian Jews in eight months, against only 19,000 from Germany itself. In Czechoslovakia 300,000 Jews had fallen into the hands of the Germans and here once more Eichmann, promoted to captain, was busy, squeezing Jews out of the country at an even higher rate than in Austria.

And in case there was any hesitation about leaving among those who could afford it, Hitler now added his personal endorsement to the predictions of Göring and *Das Schwarze Korps*. He

Čistě
ARIJSKÝ
obch

Above: Aryan shop sign in Prague. *Below:* Jews are forced to scrub the streets of Vienna; part of Austria's harassment.

told the Reichstag on 20th January 1939: 'If the international Jewish financiers . . . again succeed in plunging into world war, the result will not be the bolshevisation of the earth and thus the victory of Jewry, but the annihilation of the Jewish race throughout Europe.'

The same year had seen the consolidation of all security services under the SS into what came to be called the RSHA (*Reichssicherheitshauptamt* or Reich Main Security Office), with Heydrich as its head. It was the following year that Eichmann's talents were recognised when he was made head of Department IVA4b, that responsible for Jews, with its own four-storey building at 116 Kurfurstenstrasse.

Still the 'emigration' went on. It meant one thing: simple expulsion from all the Reich territories. Boat fares were purchased by the Jewish community at large and the emigrants left, often with very little likelihood of acceptance by the countries of destination, but in the certainty that return to Germany meant a lingering death in a concentration camp. With the assistance of the

Jewish Councils set up wherever possible (on the model of an existing one the Germans had found in Prague) it was possible to keep a permanent watch all on Jews. On 6th July 1939 the 'Tenth Decree, supplementing the Reich Citizenship Law' brought the union of Jewish relief and charity organisations in Germany itself under a department of state controlled by the RSHA. Under the same decree the remaining Jewish firms were expropriated without compensation. Deprived of their businesses, debarred from all employment except work in the forced labour battalions, which in any case could only absorb a small proportion – about a fifth, the German Jews, together with those of Austria and the 'Protectorate', those parts of the dismembered Czechoslovakian republic now under German rule, were, as had always been intended, driven into destitution and towards the ghettoes for which the way had been paved by the tenancy laws.

Already virtual prisoners of state (they could hardly be called hostages since endeavour to have them ransomed by the world in general had failed) they became actual prisoners when war was declared on Germany by Britain and France on 3rd September 1939. In fact, emigration on a limited scale to neutral countries continued among those Jews who still had the means and the contacts to gain them entrées, and even after the fall of France this went on. These wanderers of the new Diaspora spread even as far as Shanghai, where the occupying Japanese found them in 1942. For their freedom the escapers were asked a high price which sometimes went directly to the SS – for Himmler certainly regarded such deals as a legitimate source of revenue; sometimes into the pockets of corrupt RSHA officials, who provided the necessary documents, usually forged. These believers in racial purity plied their trade, under Hitler's nose, almost to the war's last day.

The movement east begins

Strangely, the outbreak of war had revived hopes in the breast of German Jewry. Many Jews now believed that the German leaders would be too preoccupied to continue persecuting them. And in a major conflict might there not be a place for them, as there had been in 1914? These hopes were not totally ill-founded for the war did bring amelioration of their lot to one small sector of the Jewish population. Such a shortage of doctors and dentists developed that it became necessary to restore many Jewish ones to general practice.

In Poland, however, where there were three million Jews, the biggest haul yet gathered into the German net, the story was immediately different. As the Germans advanced, pogroms like those of the *Kristallnacht*, though immeasurably bigger in scale, followed without even the fear of damage to German property. The local population of each Polish city, as it was entered, was encouraged to expend its feelings about defeat and occupation on its Jews. It was they, German-inspired stories had it, who brought about Poland's betrayal. And this was despite the fact that when, *in extremis*, the Polish government had offered guarantees and promises to the Jewish population it had persecuted and abused for three centuries, thousands of them had flocked to the colours and 30,000 fell in the three week battle.

Those who joined in the pogroms were the more vicious local anti-semites and criminal elements, sometimes but not invariably assisted by German army rowdies. The real force behind them, however, was no doubt Heydrich, who provided the professional riot-raisers.

Even where local inhabitants did not join in, the Nazis noted with gratification that they were less sensitive than the Germans had been at the suffering of the Jews and could witness the grossest excesses without protest. The fact was that Polish antisemitism had brought about a total separation of the two communities so that there were no Poles to speak up for their 'good Jews', a German habit on which much scorn and vituperation was poured by Himmler, Heydrich and Eichmann. Indeed, what protests there were in Poland came from Germany army circles.

If Heydrich's part as the malignant puppeteer behind the pogroms is conjectural, elements of his forces and the SS as a whole were playing more open ones. In the course of the annexation of Austria, supposedly so welcome to its citizens, it was realised that repression would have to be imposed quickly if the country was to be brought to pliant subjection. To assist this motorised task forces of the Security Police and the Security Service (SD) were formed with 'special political police duties' as their official term of reference. These mobile Action Groups (or *Einsatzgruppen*) proved their efficiency so thoroughly that they were used in the Sudentenland and in Czechoslovakia. Now they were ordered to fulfil the same duties in Poland, where their mission was

SS troops look out across the Danzig Corridor

Above and right: Warsaw's Jewish district: not yet a ghetto

German troops in Austria

outlined as 'the suppression of all elements hostile to the Reich and to Germany behind the fighting line'.

It was clear here, as elsewhere, just who were included in the 'elements hostile to the Reich'. No specific orders were given to execute Jews in Poland and as a matter of fact the lines of control were not as clearly marked out in this campaign as they were later, so that technically they came under the control of army commanders, though orders were actually being issued by Himmler. Nevertheless, the combined activities against the Jews of Poland had, by the end of 1939, produced around 250,000 casualties.

From the very beginning of the campaign mass shooting was being carried out on its own initiative by one *Einsatzgruppe*. This unit, under Lieutenant-Colonel Udo von Woyrsch,

Below and right: SD troops carry out searches in Poland

The Star of David is introduced to identify Jews

was later withdrawn at the request of the army. On 24th October an SS battalion in Wloclawek, having forced local Jews to wear a distinguishing mark (the first experiment with the yellow Star of David later to become universal), rounded up about 800 and shot many of them 'while trying to escape'.

In an earlier though smaller incident on 14th September, fifty Jews were herded into a synagogue and shot. The perpetrators of the crime – two SS men – were brought to trial, but later pardoned under a general amnesty decreed by Hitler on 4th October.

The atrocities, up to this time, appeared sporadic and betrayed no indications of a larger plan behind them. But on 21st September came the first obviously planned move: its

Hans Frank admires the view from Cracow Castle

form was the report of a secret conference over which Heydrich had presided, circulated to higher army commanders in Poland. It laid down three steps: (i) the movement of all Jews into 'communities' (a euphemism for 'ghettoes') of no fewer than 500 persons each and near railway lines; (ii) the appointment of Jewish Councils and (iii) registration of all Jews by the *Einsatzgruppen*. Jews from the Reich were to be deported into Poland – the first breath of that cold wind that was to blow through Jewry in the coming years. It is significant that Heydrich referred to these measures as 'interim' ones and there was to be, he said, a 'final objective', which would take longer to achieve. This taken in conjunction with the order to place the 'communities' near railway lines has led

Polish Jews are set to work as forced labour in a munitions plant

commentators to the conclusion that the 'final objective' was indeed the Final Solution – the total extermination of the Jews. But it must be said at this stage that this might have been to facilitate their further resettlement in a Jewish reserve to be established in Lublin.

In so far as it was possible with a war raging, there were still attempts to force Jewish emigration. Even in Poland efforts were made to push them across the line of demarcation between the German and Russian sectors – for the Russians, too, had of course marched into Poland's most easterly provinces. Large groups of Jews were driven across the river San which for part of its course marked this border. Sometimes they were lucky enough to be allowed through; some were later to be recaptured by the Germans in the war with Russia; a few managed to reach the safety of the armaments factories in the Urals and Siberia. Those who did not gain admittance had to recross the San or the Bug and were often fired at and, if not shot, allowed to drown. The few who avoided both these fates were imprisoned.

The result of German victory in Poland had been to divide that part of the country now under their control into two parts: the most westerly Polish provinces up to Lodz were incorporated into the Reich; the rest became the 'General Government', a kind of vast human dumping ground, with obviously tempting opportunities for the demographic experiments Hitler and Himmler had long dreamed of. These were on the way towards realisation through a scheme known as the 'Strengthening of German Folkdom' for which, on 12th October, Himmler was made Reichskommissar. This would entail wholesale movements of population. Germans abroad would be brought back and put in colonies in the German-incorporated territories of Poland. The Poles already there (whose land was to be used) were to be subjugated by means

as unrealistic as they were brutal, and a mass-deportation of Jews into the region of the General Government was envisaged.

The execution of Heydrich's planned regroupment of the Jews was actually slower than he imagined it would be: he was always a totally unrealistic planner. It was not, therefore, until September the following year that a general order restricting Jewish residence and thus paving the way for his ghettoes was issued. One cause of this delay was that Hans Frank, the governor appointed by Hitler to head the civilian administration of the General Government, who was now aping the medieval king in the Wawel Palace in Cracow, his new capital, shared the dislike of many Germans for the SS. This was based, in his case, not so much on humanitarian considerations, as upon jealousy for their power and influence. As soon as he learned of the plan, he protested against Himmler's intention to resettle Jews from the Reich in his fief.

On 26th October 1939 the principle of forced (and unpaid) labour for all Jews between the ages of fourteen and sixty was introduced in Poland; on 23rd November all Jews and Jewish enterprises were required to bear a distinguishing mark. In the case of individuals this was an armband with a yellow Star of David on it – it was a further two years before these distinguishing marks were introduced into the west. On 11th December a whole range of regulations were promulgated, intended to restrict the movements of Jews, and by 26th January 1940, they were debarred from using the trains – a rule which in the event proved impossible to enforce.

In the Reich-incorporated territories of Poland were some 650,000 Jews. Half a million of these, Himmler announced, were, in spite of Frank's protests, to be expelled to the General Government. He was as good as his word and the deportation began

BENUTZUNG DURCH JUDEN VERBOTEN
UZYWANIE TEGO WOZU ŻYDOM WZBRONIONE

'Jews not allowed'

before the end of the year 1939 and
continued until the following March,
though there had been a temporary
interruption in January when Frank's
civil administration had been joined
in its protests by the army's Economics and Armaments Office. These
protests by the army, based on the
fact that the deportations were
depriving them of skilled personnel in
Germany, were to continue and were
at first taken at face value by Heydrich and Himmler. Later, they
realised the army was using this as
an excuse to save Jews from the fate
planned for them. At this time,
however, the army was not the only
source of protest. Other representations were made by the officials of
the State Railways, who claimed
that the demands being made on
them were too great in view of other
war needs – an argument not without
justification, particularly later.

The main General Government
reception area for the deportees
was at this time round Lublin, the
site of the Jewish 'reserve' – another
of the projects talked of, begun and
then abandoned. In this case it was
dropped early in 1940 because it was
soon shown to be impracticable for
such large numbers.

Not all the Jews now travelling
eastwards came from 'Reich' Poland.
Some came from Czechoslovakia,
Austria and even Germany itself.
The numbers were already too high
for the areas involved to absorb
them – a matter which elicited further
protest on purely administrative
grounds from Frank, and on humanitarian ones from the Army Commander in the East, Field-Marshal
Blaskowitz. Many people, he reported,
were dying of hunger in the reception
villages; children were arriving in
the deportation trains frozen to death.
Notwithstanding this, Hitler told an
American newspaper correspondent,
after the abandonment of the scheme,
that to found a Jewish state on Lublin
would force them to 'live in such
overcrowded conditions it would be
impossible for them to attain a
tolerable standard of living'.

A more terrible fate awaited German Jews who were moved from areas such as Stettin and Schneidermuhl to the General Government zone in mid-winter. Something like 1,360 were forced to march for fourteen hours through snow. By March, 230 were dead, many of those who perished being young children. That the Germans were far from insensitive to world opinion in this is shown by the speed and vehemence with which they denied any rumours of these deportations and their cost to the deportees, which reached the neutral press. They were also worried about reports of their activities reaching the Russians, whose attitudes in such matters they were unsure of.

Once in Lublin, Himmler had plans of his own for the migrants. Since the 1938 *Anschluss* which had brought large numbers of political dissidents into the concentration camps, Himmler and several of his associates had been concerned about deriving some benefit from this potential, but unused, labour capacity. Among the immediate proposals were brickmaking (thus imitating the Jews' early Egyptian slave-masters), and quarrying, although as ambition grew within the Nazi leadership, far more elaborate projects were conceived. Himmler, for example, was anxious to build up sources of revenue for the SS should it cease to be the apple of his Führer's eye. But none of the far-reaching schemes instituted or talked about was ever fully realised, largely because for many people, not least of all Heydrich, forced-labour was just another way of destroying unwanted bodies.

Nevertheless, Odilo Globocnik, head of the SS and Chief of Police in Lublin, began organising the forced-labour on what he saw as promising and profitable lines. At the same time the traffic in Jews became two-way as some 57,000 of them, considered as fit for work, were brought to Germany in the first six weeks of Occupation. Many were employed in the Wehr-

Odilo Globocnik, head of the SS and chief of police in Lublin

macht's own ordnance factories.

Major-General Globocnik, a semiliterate, drunken lout with a talent for deceit and conspiracy, was to use Jewish labour in partnership with various German entrepreneurs as corrupt as himself and amass a fortune before his final dismissal. He saw the General Government and particularly Lublin as a special field for his talents.

With all these schemes, therefore, there had commenced the deportation and 'resettlement' programme, the callous movement and deposition of human souls which was to continue to the last moment of the war.

There were and would remain a series of carefully graduated steps in the German treatment of the Jews. Emigration and deportation represented one, and the Jews now within the General Government were being forced, partly by external pressures intended to have this effect and partly from the herd instinct which manifests itself most strongly in times of

Above and right : The Warsaw ghetto, 1940

disaster, into the second phase: enclosure in ghettoes.

The first of these to be established was in Warsaw. The area chosen, in keeping with the Nazi taste for the traditional, was one which had included the site of the medieval ghetto, and also, since there were more Jews in Warsaw now than in the middle ages, part of the city's former industrial area, including its railway station. At first the intention of this 'resettlement' was disguised as quarantine – the prevention of contagious diseases to which Jews were supposed to be more prone than others. So in September 1940 the quarantine zone enclosed besides 240,000 Jews, 80,000 gentile Poles behind its barbed wire and fencing. The following month the quarantine excuse was dropped and the Poles were ordered out. In their place another 120,000 Jews were moved in. There were now 360,000 people in a place intended for 160,000.

Similar ghettoes were established in other cities under control of the General Government: Cracow, Lublin, Radom and Lwow. It had been seriously supposed that once this had been done the ghetto population could be exterminated by destitution and starvation. This proved impractical for two reasons: firstly, although in Germany, Austria and Czechoslovakia Jews nowhere represented more than one to two per cent of the total population, in Poland they represented ten per cent and in some individual towns as much as twenty-five per cent. Despite their segregation from the inhabitants as a whole they had learned many different trades and skills and so were able to provide ghetto services in a way which astonished their persecutors, who had allowed themselves to be taken in by their own propaganda of the Jew as a parasitical sharp trader and

Typhus is proclaimed as the excuse to isolate the ghetto

Above: Lublin ghetto, 1941. *Left:* Lwow ghetto, 1942

Food is smuggled over the wall into the ghetto

speculator. But the Polish Jews, placed in a society largely hostile to them, had become past-masters in the arts of survival, contributing a great deal to the general community. Thus when it came to the practical implementation of anti-semitism the less-organised hostility of the Poles wavered. The measures they had at first welcomed began to cause real deprivation by denying them the talents they themselves needed for survival under a repressive occupation. (As Slavonic Poles they were only one rung higher in the German racial ladder and Poles and Jews were normally bracketed together in German resettlement plans.) Without realising it they had grown dependent on Jewish skills and they began to feel less enthusiasm even for this one aspect of Nazi policy they had hitherto been prepared to accept.

Jewish workers leave a factory within the ghetto

All the same, the starvation policy was tried and led to countless deaths, but even after introducing summary executions for any Jews caught outside the ghetto or who approached too close to its barbed wire, trading with the outer world could not be stopped. In this the SS guards themselves proved far from incorruptible.

Amid extreme difficulties some semblance of an administration in the ghetto was imposed by the Jewish Council. To begin with there were services, including schools and hospitals, black market restaurants, cafés, nightclubs and brothels, these last luxuries being maintained largely through the assistance of the Gestapo whose members made a handsome profit on the trade involved. The Germans even allowed in parcels sent from abroad at this time, though this facility was later stopped and in the end all mail from the ghetto was refused by the German post office, which gave as its reasons for these measures 'the fear of epidemics'.

The deterioration of ghetto life became increasingly marked as its numbers increased through the resettlement of more and more Reich and other Jews. There were factories in the ghetto and some outside to which Jews were allowed to go each day, but they were incapable of supplying employment for the large numbers now involved. Soup kitchens were set up through the Jewish Council, but these, at times driven to making soup from hay, in the end were forced to close. Death from malnutrition and starvation became commonplace. The bodies of the dead were found lying on the streets daily, generally stripped naked so that others might use their rags as clothing.

In these circumstances, fear of a plague constantly haunted the Germans: if ghetto deaths exceeded the capacity of the burial services, what then? Furthermore, vast increases in the numbers of Jews coming east could be expected if Göring lifted, as he was expected to, a ban he had placed on deportations following a story about them in a

Death in the Warsaw ghetto quickly becomes commonplace

Swiss newspaper. Morever there were other ways in which the numbers might soon be substantially raised. The invasion of Denmark and Norway in the spring of 1940, then of France and the Low Countries, had brought all these countries, with their Jewish populations, within the ambit of German administration.

Heydrich and his department were never far behind events, however, and as an ambitious man he no doubt welcomed the vast increments to his empire, despite the problems they brought – for in six weeks following 10th May 1940, 350,000 Jews fell into German hands, of whom about 120,000 were refugees from Germany itself. Heydrich's first reaction, faced by this, was to use the Vichy zone of France, unoccupied by the terms of the armistice, for their 'resettlement', in the way that the General Government of Poland had been used as a dumping ground. In consequence no impediment was placed in the way of those who sought to leave the Occupied Zone to go there. This continued after the Vichy Government promulgated a 'Statut des Juifs' on 4th October 1940, which ordered the interning of Jewish refugees (the indigenous population, as French citizens, enjoyed the protection of the law); 40,000 such Jews were interned in camps at Gurs, Les Milles and Rivesaltes, and thereby deprived of liberty and civil rights Heydrich exceeded himself by slipping 7,450 Reich Jews, many of whom died on the journey, into the Unoccupied Zone on 22nd October, but the French, fearing a large increase in this practice, protested forcefully enough to stop further movement.

Hitler was so fanatical a believer in a chimera of Jewish international conspiracies that he hoped the western Jews who had fallen into his hands might be used as hostages to

Funeral vehicles in Warsaw. Demands on burial services soon exceeded capacity

Baldur von Schirach

Dr Franz Six

circumvent them. Indeed, hostages were another of his obsessions and at one stage in the war he deported English-born families from the Channel Islands with the intention that they should be hostages against British bombing of the Reich, by distributing them in the bigger cities. The European Jews, of this earlier scheme, could – he seriously believed – be held in Lublin or at some other place where they would constitute guarantees of the 'good behaviour' of American Jews. The plan came to nothing.

Heydrich, now debarred from dumping Jews in Vichy France, was trying to introduce the classical pattern of organising the Jewish population in the Occupied Zone, by consolidating the charity organisations and establishing Jewish councils. The tactic never worked as it had worked in other places largely because the French Government officials whose cooperation was essential lacked either the stomach or the zeal for the preservation of the racial purity of their occupiers. No

French Jew would lend his name to the Jewish Councils, and even in pro-Vichy circles there was a willingness to help Jews, while naturalised French Jews continued to be regarded as French citizens. The only people the Germans could lay their hands on were those refugees who had not been long enough in the country to take out naturalisation papers. The Germans wanted at all costs to make it appear that the French had turned spontaneously on their Jews and were treating them as they had been treated in Germany, Austria, Czechoslovakia and Poland. In this they were constantly thwarted, and because of their frustration, though attempts were made and some Jews were ruthlessly executed, persecution of Jews in France failed to take place on any scale.

In other parts of occupied Europe Heydrich's office was proceeding in various ways, during the days following German victory, to put into operation the progressive steps of its measures, trying to bring their new acquisitions into an overall

78

Lieutenant-Colonel Rudolf Höss, Commandant of Auschwitz

schedule. They met with varying success. This had little to do with the national attitudes to the Jews. Almost everywhere in northern and western Europe there was a lack of enthusiasm for Jew-baiting, and even in Germany, whose people had been subjected to eight years of Nazi propaganda, there was much apathy and moral cowardice in the face of vile injustice, but much detestation for it. So throughout the war there were German families who hid Jews and they included all sections of society, among them at least one family of Prussian aristocrats, whose head was an active general of the Wehrmacht.

The success or failure of Heydrich's endeavours in occupied Europe tended to reflect the type of occupation the country was undergoing and the sort of Jewish organisation which existed in it before. Thus, in Holland, where, unlike France, the whole government of the country was under German supervision with a puppet Dutch government dancing to its tune, the rounding up and subsequent deportation of Jews was almost totally successful, despite the prohibition the Cardinal Archbishop put on Catholic police officers participating in this activity (their refusal often cost them their jobs), and the universal loathing felt by Dutch people for this kind of persecution. Neighbouring Belgium was in the hands of a military administration and its governor, General von Falkenhausen, was an outspoken opponent of National Socialism. Here, fewer than a third of the country's Jews were rounded up. Denmark and Norway were different again. Denmark was a neutral country under German occupation. Norway, though ruled by a Reichskommissar like Holland, was adjacent to neutral Sweden, which throughout the war left its door ajar to Jewish refugees, even organising and distributing Swedish naturalisation papers openly in Norway through its consulate. This, helped by the facts that the Jewish population was small, and the Norwegians were opposed like the Dutch to antisemitism, helped to forestall Heydrich's aims.

These are exceptions in an almost totally dismal story.

Its dismal character is scarcely alleviated by the absurdity of many of the Nazi plans. One of these was the revival of the Madagascar Project of 1938. With France, to whom the island belonged, under occupation, the Germans believed that such a plan was a possibility and proposed to send there the 'western Jews' who were to be kept as international hostages. Feasibility studies were therefore begun by Adolf Eichmann in the summer of 1940 and lasted nearly a year. With the seas patrolled by the British navy the possibility of moving 4,000,000 people – the number projected – to an offshore island of the African continent can never have looked very viable. No one knew, for instance, where Germany was to find the ships with which to undertake this project.

A second plan also canvassed at this time, but never seriously investigated, was for a Jewish National Home in Palestine. This was spiked with still greater difficulties. Palestine was still in British hands and the British administration there had made clear that it would accept no more than a trickle of refugees for fear of offending the Arabs, a policy which was to contribute vastly (as it had already contributed) to Jewish sufferings, both before and after the war. Furthermore, it was felt that this might lead to Palestine becoming a kind of Judaic Vatican.

Neither plan materialised, though the Palestine project was kept alive to the extent that rumours of it would be dropped into the ghettoes from time to time, giving those becoming desperate an empty hope.

The view that both plans amounted to no more than a 'cover story' is supported by two witnesses: Himmler (reported at second hand by his masseur, Felix Kersten) and Baldur von Schirach, *gauleiter* of Vienna. Hitler saw both these men in the summer of 1940; Himmler at about the time of the fall of France. To von Schirach, the Führer confided that he intended to resettle the Viennese Jews in the General Government, but to Himmler he gave the task of the progressive extermination of the European Jews. If the Madagascar project was referred to at all at this meeting it must have been summarily dismissed. Himmler's instruction was given the formal seal of a Führer Order during the ensuing months, athough it was never committed to paper and was revealed only by stages to those involved.

There were from the outset to be two prime instruments of destruction: 'natural diminution' (Heydrich's happy term) through killingly hard work in forced labour gangs; and the liquidation of those surviving in concentration camps assigned and equipped for the task. A third method introduced into plans subsequently was through the *Einsatzgruppen* of the SD, whose role of 'cleansing' areas behind the army was to be given a wider connotation. A number of groups were set up, one, headed by SS Colonel Professor Dr Franz Six, former head of the Economics Faculty at the University of Berlin, was appointed to control the Action Group to be sent to Britain after invasion. Training in special crash courses was given at Prezsch, near Leipzig.

As to the other methods of destruction, sites for the extermination camps had already been chosen and one, Auschwitz, began functioning as a normal concentration camp in the spring of 1940. Others were to be at Treblinka, Sobibor, Chelmno and Belsec – all except Chelmno in the General Government. To liquidate the Jews of the Lublin 'reserve' there would be facilities at the labour camp Majdanek.

The commandant Himmler had appointed to Auschwitz, Lieutenant-Colonel Rudolf Höss, was a man after his own heart: full of plans as grandiose as they were unrealistic, including one to establish an agricultural research station in the camp, which would specialise in plant and stock breeding.

Besides locations both techniques and personnel were needed for the mass-killings and the disposal of bodies (this in particular was to cause a problem). But in the matter of skills the Germans had some expertise to call upon. Since 1939 gassing had been used for dispatching those condemned as incurable under the euthanasia programme. Hitler, as his *Mein Kampf* comment on Jews indicates, having been gassed himself in the First World War, had a fixation about the subject. The methods used in the euthanasia institutes had included even coal gas. Hitler, in deference to public opinion, was to bring the euthanasia programme to an end in August 1941 – though it continued under a different guise.

This, however, meant that the institute staffs were to be available for the extermination of the Jews. Indeed, they were already being used for the purpose as those unfit for work were sent off to the nearest 'institute' on a one way ticket. Their numbers reached such proportions that this led to a testy protest from the director of one institute about overwork.

While all these preparations were being made, inside Germany and throughout Occupied Europe there was a tightening up of anti-Jewish measures. In France, Holland and Belgium the registration of Jews was embarked upon; the Polish ghettoes were walled up.

These measures were for the most part carried out without incident. But not entirely. In February 1941, German police with Dutch collaborationist militia began raiding houses in the Jewish quarter of Amsterdam, because, it was claimed, shots had been fired from a window. When they saw what was going on Dutch workers from a nearby factory poured out to help the Jews and in the melée a Dutch militiaman was killed. Further riots occurred when the Germans mounted a massive funeral for the dead man. 390 Jews, all young men, were arrested as hostages, whereupon a general strike spread through the city. The Germans were forced to rush in police and SS troops from Germany. Sixty Dutchmen were sent to concentration camps and with them the 390 Jewish hostages. Most of them had died before the end of the year.

As part of the same tightening up process, on 14th May 3,600 Paris Jews were interned – an act which caused deep anger in Vichy and led to many subsequent problems for those Germans who had day-to-day dealings with the Pétain government.

Graveyard of a mental hospital; the outcome of the euthanasia programme

The massacres

Amid Europe-wide activity on the part of RSHA and particularly department IVA4b, the military planners were also busily engaged. In the last three months of 1940, they were laying down, in the deepest secrecy, the strategy for an attack on Russia to take place the following year. Hitler, we now know, believed Britain to be disabled as a belligerent force and accordingly felt able to rid himself of his last potential enemy on the European continent and at the same time carry to finality his long-cherished dream of extirpating Bolshevism.

For Himmler this promised vast new problems, but also vast new opportunities: problems in that he had the duty of dismantling the the Soviet system and policing the occupied areas; opportunities, in that this new territory would provide vast new dumping grounds and in a region far enough removed from metropolitan Germany to allow much greater freedom of action.

For policing four *Einsatzgruppen* were formed, designated A, B, C and D. The total number of these groups was under 3,000, including specialists, such as radio operators and interpreters (some of whom were women). They broke up into units or *Kommandos* of between 600 and 900 each.

The lesson of Poland where the Action Groups were technically subservient to the army command had been learned and clear demarcations of control were agreed. The *Einsatzgruppen* were subordinate to the army in regard to movement, rations and billeting, but to Heydrich for discipline, jurisdiction and technical matters. In other words, Heydrich issued the orders. The army had insisted on a clause whereby they could give orders to Action Groups near the front line, though even this right was severely circumscribed.

Otto Ohlendorf, a handsome intellectual, trained lawyer and economist who joined the SD in 1936, described under oath how he had been briefed by Himmler when he was appointed to command one of the groups: 'Himmler stated that an important part of our task consisted in the extermination of Jews – men, women and children – and of Communist functionaries'. Ohlendorf was himself responsible for exterminating 90,000 men, women and children.

Some time in June 1941, Himmler ordered Rudolf Höss, the Auschwitz commandant, to 'prepare installations at Auschwitz where mass exterminations could take place'. He was further told that Eichmann would visit him there and give him detailed instructions. Before Eichmann's visit

Otto Ohlendorf

Höss went to the newly established camp at Treblinka where gassings were already being carried out in a permanent chamber which used carbon monoxide gas generated from internal combustion engines. He came back with a poor opinion of this and was to tell Eichmann when he arrived in July that it was 'quite out of the question' to use such methods for mass-extermination.

While Höss was absent from the camp his security chief, Captain Fritzsch, tried experimenting with Zyklon B crystals, a form of prussic acid used for fumigation. Höss repeated the experiment on a larger scale. 850 prisoners, 600 of them Russian prisoners of war, were locked in a cellar and the crystals thrown in. Twelve hours later the cellar was opened up, but among the bodies packed so tight they could not fall in death, were some still alive on whom the process had to be repeated.

Entrance to a 'shower'

Can of Zyklon B

It had been suggested that it would be politic not to have the extermination centre in the main camp itself and in fact the gas chambers first used were two converted barns in a camp at Birkenwald nearby. They could not, in total, take more than 250 victims, so that bigger chambers had to be designed and built. Of these Höss was particularly proud.

It is said they were designed by Paul Blobel, a drunken Dusseldorf architect, soon to distinguish himself as a commander of an Action Group *Kommando*. It was, however, another ingenious planner who made these chambers look like shower rooms, complete with douches in the ceiling. In some place victims were even provided, to give verisimilitude to the deception, with a cake of soap – in fact a small block of cement, afterwards recovered from dead hands to be passed to the next candidate for cleansing.

The first massive anti-Jewish action of the war – perhaps what was needed to convince the more cautious Germans that such things did not inevitably bring down the wrath of humanity on their heads – came from the third and perhaps least significant of the three nations which at Evian in 1938 had stated its desire to be rid of its Jews – Rumania. The country had its equivalent of the Nazis – the Iron Guard. They had helped to make Rumania an ally of Germany in the war on Russia. On 22nd June three German army groups began their thrusts into Russia, one of them by way of Rumania. Two days later the town of Jassy was heavily bombed by the Russians. The Iron Guardists, who had already massacred Jews in Bucharest and exposed their bodies in the city's kosher butchers' shops, now turned on those of Jassy. The Jews were rounded up during the night of

Gas chamber at Dachau

Antonescu, dictator of Rumania

It was not long after this, in early July, that Heydrich received an official commission from Göring 'to carry out all preparations . . . for a total solution on the Jewish question'. He was further authorised to submit a report on measures so far taken for the execution of the 'final solution of the Jewish question' – the first recorded use of the phrase. At his trial before the Nuremberg War Crimes Tribunal Göring was to dispute the meaning of those last six words. Heydrich appeared to be in no doubt about it. For on 20th May 1941 a decree was issued by RSHA to German police and SD representatives in Belgium and France. This brought to an end emigration outside the occupied territories as well as 'resettlement' in the east. The reason for this was stated to be 'the certain final solution of the Jewish problem' shortly to be applied. The 'Final Solution' thus became the code name for extermination.

28th June. The next day intermittent and summary executions took place. Then some 5,000 were loaded on a train, 120 to a wagon, bound for Bucharest, 300 miles away. The train never reached the city, but after two days meandering round the country-side, during which at various stops dead bodies were thrown out, it reached a remote station in the Carpathian foothills. By this time only 1,000 of the original number were still alive. If to the 4,000 who perished on the train are added some 3,000 killed in the streets and during the round up then some 7,000 Jews had lost their lives

Hitler spoke with the warmest approval of this action: 'A man . . . like Antonescu', he said of the Rumanian dictator, 'proceeds in these matters in a far more radical fashion than we have up to the present.' Thus, the Rumanian killers were held up as an example for German emulation and as implied criticism of their reticence.

A minute circulated by Göring to his four higher SS and police officers began to put into effect his commission. This underlined Himmler's brief to Ohlendorf: that part of their task was to exterminate Jews and Communist functionaries. A final paragraph instructed them not to interfere with any anti-Communist or anti-Jewish measures initiated by local people, but, on the contrary, to encourage them secretly, while being sure that such encouragement could not be attributed to the occupiers. Its last sentence adds a warning: 'Special care should be taken in regard to the shooting of doctors and others engaged in medical practice. . .'

The instruction to encourage local talent was quickly put into effect. In Lithuania, liberated from the Soviet Union by the *Wehrmacht* early in the war, bands of thugs roamed the streets killing some 3,800 local Jews in the capital Kovno alone, before the German army stepped in to stop such activities, Even after this, on

4th July, only two days after Heydrich's orders had been promulgated, Lithuanian partisans under German instructions shot 416 Jews, including nearly fifty women, outside Kovno.

Heydrich's man on the spot, Brigadier-General Franz Stahlecker, commander of *Einsatzgruppe* A, saw other ways in which local anti-semitism and its violent manifestations could be turned to their benefit. He had the Jews confined in a ghetto – for their 'own protection' – and when he found the one designated for the purpose too small solved his accommodation problem by executing all the Jews unfit for work in batches of fifty to a hundred. These killings were repeated six days later when 700 hostages taken in Vilna were executed outside the town at petrol storage tank pits thoughtfully dug by the Red Army at Ponary. Pit executions of this kind were to become a feature of the application of the Final Solution in Russia and the Baltic

and this site itself was used again and again. The second such occasion was in September, allegedly after the shooting of two German soldiers, when 700 hostages were executed. By the end of the year 30,000 Jews had died in this place. In the meantime at Kovno 10,000 people were shot in a single day and then a further 10,000 at Dvinsk.

During November and December 24,000 people were taken in motor buses to execution sites in Riga. Here, however, the action was seen by regular troops who brought back accounts of the killings to Germany. There were to be many more such occasions.

The process used at Kovno became the classic pattern of destruction of Jews by *Einsatzgruppen*. The Jewish population of a town would be enclosed in ghettoes – in practice any group of buildings which could be found irrespective of their suitability

Russian Jews are put to menial tasks

for sustained human habitation. The ghetto had its own internal government, a Jewish Council, whose functions including making arrangements for those to be 'resettled', which by this time meant executed. Those first resettled would invariably be the unemployed, sick and orphans. Reitlinger has indentified four stages in the history of the Nazi ghettoes. When first introduced they were intended only to stop Jews from trading. Secondly, they became places where the Jews were left to die of hunger. The third stage was that in which non-essential Jews were executed. The last was yet to come: the total destruction of the ghettoes and their razing to the ground.

Details of the method of execution in use at this time were also given by Ohlendorf in the trial statement quoted earlier: 'The unit selected . . . would enter a village or city and order prominent Jewish citizens to call together all Jews for the purpose of resettlement. They were requested to hand over their valuables . . . and shortly before execution to surrender their outer clothing. The men, women and children were led to a place of execution which in most cases was located next to a more deeply excavated antitank ditch. Then they were shot, kneeling or standing, and the corpses thrown into the ditch. . .'

Nor were the executioners by any means always limited to the *Einsatzgruppen* members. We know that local antisemites as well as the locally-recruited police helped in the killings. We also know that German civilians, doing such jobs as interpreting, and even railwaymen, volunteered to join the firing squads because there was plunder to be had and a special ration of schnapps. With killers so untrained it is no wonder that it was the exception rather than the rule for victims to be dispatched outright. Many, perhaps the majority, died not from shooting but from suffocation caused by the weight of bodies on top of them or

of the soil when the grave was filled in, and even from drowning in their own and other people's blood. It was unusual, the day after an action, not to find a trail of dead and dying outside the grave. Some actually turned up for hospital treatment and a few escaped altogether.

The massacres continued: at Korosten, at Berdichev, at Uman, at Winnitsa in the western Ukraine; at Zhitomir 2,531 Jews died in the last week of July, another 407 in early August and some 1,668 in early September. And later in that same month there occurred the blackest of all the massacres by the Action Groups. This was in Kiev which fell to the Germans on the 19th.

Five days after occupation the headquarters of the Rear Area Command of the Sixth Army in the Continental Hotel was destroyed in an explosion, obviously from a booby-trapped mine left by the Russians, Hundreds of German troops died fighting the subsequent fires.

It was decided that reprisals should fall upon the Jews. SS Colonel Paul Blobel, head of *Kommando* 4a of *Einsatzgruppe* C, that same Blobel who, allegedly, designed the Auschwitz gas-chambers, was given the task of carrying out the executions.

On 26th September therefore Kiev Jews were ordered to report within three days for 'resettlement'. No more than 5,000 to 6,000 were expected to obey the summons. Actually, 'thanks to an extremely clever organisation', in the words of an *Einsatzgruppe* daily report, 30,000 arrived carrying their bundles. Two further reports put the figure at nearer to 34,000.

The place of execution was the Babi Yar ravine just outside Kiev. Here as they stepped from a plank into the ravine they were killed with a shot in the back of the neck. The operation took two days.

The executioners deceived themselves that the population in general knew nothing of the liquidations. It

Partisans are executed in Russia

was public knowledge and only terror can have kept people from talking about it in such a way that the Germans would have learned of their knowledge. The massacre was later to form the subject of Russian poet Yevgeny Yevtushenko's lament.

The invasion of Russia had, of necessity, brought Galicia, which had been part of Poland since 1919 and annexed by the Soviets in 1939, into the sphere of Nazi influence. Here, as in the Baltic, measures against the Jews were quickly instituted and local forces encouraged to participate in pogroms in one of which, at Lwow, 7,000 Jews were killed during what was called 'Aktion Petlura'.

Further massacres took place in Kiev in October and January 1942, in which a total of 15,000 people perished. At Dniepropetrovsk, on 13th October 1941, 11,000 children and old people were killed in a single action. At Borissov, a week later, all the town's 7,620 Jews were killed by *Einsatzgruppe* A; on 6th November 15,000 at Rowno, in the Ukraine. During December massacres at Riga, Vilna and Simferopol in the Crimea were completed accounting for 70,000. In four months 350,000, in all, had been shot.

The executions were always disguised as actions against potential partisans or their sympathisers. The credibility of this is destroyed by the fact one *Kommando* of an *Einsatzgruppe* reported shooting Jewish children almost daily and in one action, on 29th August 1941, executed 1,469 of them. *Einsatzgruppe* A which had already executed 229,052 Jews, reported by November 1941 that though it had killed only fifty-six partisans, plus 1,064 Communists, it had shot 126,421 Jews. Still further destructive evidence comes from Ohlendorf. In the Crimea the members of two Jewish sects had been rounded up. One was of Muslims converted to Judaism; the other of Jews converted to Muslimism. The first sect was spared, on, Ohlendorf discovered,

the orders of Department IVA4b; the second, as racial Jews, was destroyed, thereby proving that it was on racial grounds and not the question of their adherence to the partisans (which was never raised) that settled their fate.

The shooting of children was an act which no one could be persuaded partook of the character of anti-partisan activity. To dispose of them more discreetly gas-vans were introduced. These were vehicles so adapted that at a touch of a lever the carbon monoxide generated in the exhaust fumes was fed into the passenger compartment. The victims were conveyed from prison or ghetto to place of burial in the van and were supposed to be extinct on arrival, a neat if macabre economy. The intention was not always fulfilled – though the innovators of the system were inclined to blame the vans' drivers rather than themselves for this failure. The use of gassing vans drew protests from the members of *Einsatzgruppen* themselves on the ground that the cruelties involved were morally indefensible. Since a letter giving instructions on the proper use of the vans speaks of corpses smeared with excrement and with their faces contorted from suffocation (as opposed to the painless gas asphyxia the vans were supposed to induce), one can understand how it turned even these hardened stomachs. Nevertheless, their use continued and was even extended.

If horror at what was being done appeared to focus itself round points of detail rather than principle this is not completely the case, though indignation and revulsion did not anywhere achieve a volume proportional to its causes. Disgust was freely expressed, for example, by ordinary soldiers, among whom it must be remembered were many who had been through an indoctrination in antisemitism in the Hitler Youth. In consequence Field-

Field-Marshal Walter von Reichenau

Marshal Walter von Reichenau, commander of the Sixth Army, felt compelled to offer some justification for what was being done. 'The soldier in the Eastern Territories,' he declared in an Order-of-the-Day on 10th October 1941, 'is not merely a fighter according to the rules of the art of war, but also the bearer of a ruthless national ideology... Therefore, the soldier must have understanding of the necessity of a severe but just revenge on sub-human Jewry'. Nevertheless, in an official report written in December 1941, a staff officer in the Army Group Centre declared that the officer corps 'almost to a man, is against the shooting of Jews, prisoners and commissars'. They saw it, the same writer said, as a stain upon the German army.

A member of the army's economics bureau in the Ukraine wrote that there was 'no evidence that the Jews were widely engaged in sabotage or similar acts', nor could they be considered 'to represent a threat to the German *Wehrmacht*'. A stronger expression of feeling came from Reichskommissar Wilhelm Kube, a founder-member of the NSDAP, who had already demonstrated his loathing for these excesses and was being watched on Heydrich's behalf by the Gestapo. He wrote to Himmler of 'indescribable brutality' and of 'extreme beastliness' and described how a young Jewish girl was asked for 5,000 roubles as the price for her father's life and begun rushing everywhere begging for money. Such uneasiness was ignored and by the spring of 1942 at least a million Jews had perished in these actions.

Yet by no means all the Jews in these regions had been killed. The residue remained in the ghettoes with all their apparatus of Jewish Councils and with their inmates forced to wear the yellow star on chest and back. They were ordered to be given only the minimum of food, that available when the rest of the population had been fed and 'in no case more than was sufficient to sustain life'.

A key-appointment was made in September – a step towards the ultimate destruction of the ghettoes. This gave Eichmann, in addition to his other functions, charge of transport organisation. His brief covered not only movement eastward but also that from the occupied western and northern parts of Europe. Here, too, progress in the Final Solution was being made, though in many places with a tardiness Heydrich and his RSHA found exasperating and deplorable.

In October, with Eichmann in his new office, deportations from the Reich and beyond were going on apace. Goods trains, loaded with 1,000 people drawn from Berlin, Hamburg, Hanover, Dortmund, Düsseldorf, Cologne, Frankfurt, Kassel, Stutt-

A further load of deportees leaves for the camp

Russian Jews murdered by Soviet troops in the Ukraine

gart, Nuremberg, Munich and Breslau, besides Vienna, Prague, Luxembourg and even Antwerp were steaming east. The deportations continued until January 1942 to areas which included Lodz, Warsaw, Kovno, Minsk and Riga. In these deportations the consolidated Jewish charity and relief organisations – the Reich Union – and the Jewish Councils were forced to help by providing lists for 'resettlement'.

In 1941, the United States was still neutral and a reporter of the *New York Times* approached close enough to witness the departure of one train-load and duly filed his story. The deportations were also public knowledge in Berlin, at least, and caused such revulsion that party leaders were forced to distribute leaflets among the crowd denouncing Jewish 'guilt'.

Even so Gentiles began putting on the Star of David, which the Jews of Berlin had been compelled to wear only a month before – two years from its first use in Poland. At a sermon in St Hedwig's Cathedral, on the Sunday following one of the departures, the elderly Catholic Provost Lichtenberg said he wished to be sent east to share the fate of the Jews. He got, not his wish, but death in a concentration camp.

None knew what the deportees would meet on arrival. Those bound for Kovno and Riga in one transport chanced to arrive while a 'special action' – that is a mass-shooting – was in progress and were dragged from the train to join the other victims. Others, temporarily spared, found overfilled and starving ghettoes to whose inhabitants their arrival was scarely welcome. Frank, the governor, was furious about the restarting of the 'resettlements' and in no mood to show magnaminity to those who were adding to his burdens.

It might be supposed, with all this

Ration card from the Warsaw ghetto

activity, that there would be little time or energy left to harass the remaining Jews of Germany. This was far from the case. The assault upon their lives and liberties, from every quarter, which had begun in 1933, seemed to redouble in ferocity between 1941 and the end of 1942, and, whereas in peace-time the effects, though unpleasant, were limited, it now began to impose hideous hardship. Since 1940, shopping hours for Jews had been restricted to between four and five o'clock in the afternoon when, in other words, shops were empty of the 'extras' which made survival on rations possible. In Berlin, since June 1941, they had special ration cards marked with a 'J'. They could not use public transport without a police permit and they were not allowed to use the telephone, to visit restaurants or station waiting rooms or to go into the countryside. They had to surrender woollen and fur clothing – even the fur collars off coats: they had to surrender bicycles, typewriters, records, binoculars, radios and paint their homes with the Star of David. Their own schools were closed and they were still banned from other schools. Finally, in October 1942, their egg, meat, cereal and milk rations were cancelled.

In every sector of existence preparations were being made, therefore, for 'the certain final solution of the Jewish problem'. And while in Russia and Poland the *Einsatzgruppen* were carrying out their bloody tasks, the extermination camps were being set up; two, Belsec and Chelmno, had been started in October 1941.

Yet there remained three basic problems. The first was one which in a sense, Himmler had created for himself by his desire to make the concentration camps self-supporting ventures and contributors to the German war-economy. Not only was his slave-labour being used, gratefully in view of the general shortage of labour in Germany, but in some fields in which Jewish people alone were the specialists they were in a position which made them seem indispensable. There were, for example, the diamond-cutters of Amsterdam; the furriers and leather workers of Poland, all of whom were now supplying the *Wehrmacht's* needs. What was to happen to all these?

It was made clear in a way which – in view of the pressing needs of the economy – makes explicit the manic nature of Nazi antisemitism. Nothing must interfere with unimpeded progress towards the 'solution'. In December 1941, Hinrich Lohse, *Reichskommissar* for Ostland (the name given to the occupied Russian territories) asked whether skilled workers in the *Wehrmacht's* factories were to be liquidated. He was told that 'The rules relating to the problem require that the demands of the economy be ignored.' In the end Göring, hardly a man to be suspected of sympathising with the Jews, had to intervene personally to prevent disruption of the war-effort. Even his efforts could produce only a twelve-month reprieve. The following year the army were forced to exchange trained Jewish workers for untrained Poles, but only after General von Gienath, Military District commander in the General Government, had been relieved of his command.

The second problem was that of

Hinrich Lohse

the remaining rights of German Jews under the law. The Eleventh Supplementary Decree to the Reich citizenship Law issued on 25th November 1941 took care of that. Under it Jews outside the Reich became stateless, while those within became stateless as soon as they crossed its borders – even if dragged across against their will. Thereafter they had no rights at law.

The last problem facing those directly concerned with the Final Solution was that of implicating others. Himmler and Heydrich knew themselves to be in the position of Hitler's hired assassins. They were no doubt acutely conscious of the fate of hired assassins when once their work had been done. They wanted therefore to be in the position where they could say: 'Not we alone, but all these others share our guilt; these men who now sit in their offices so respectably, they too were party to what we did'.

To this question, in the last weeks of 1941, Heydrich addressed himself.

The destruction of the ghettoes

For historians 1942 will always be the crucial year of the war, It was the year that marked the opening of Stalingrad; the year of Alamein; the year in which America threw her might into the fray. The year in which the tide turned.

These events did not go unmarked by the Jews of Europe, listening clandestinely to the BBC on receivers in the ghettoes or reading between the lines of propaganda victories in the German-run papers. If it gave them hope it was hope that was to prove hollow – for it was that same year in which, notwithstanding the mass-murders in the east during the previous one, extermination became a reality. In retrospect it is easy to jump to the conclusion that Hitler, perceiving the course of events, was determined on one thing: that if nothing else was achieved his prophecy of 1941 must be fulfilled. Jewry would be annihilated. This, instead of his thousand-year Reich, would be his monument. Yet, as has been shown, the enactment of the Final Solution was no sudden thing, but a step-by-step descent carried out to a timed strategy and its beginnings could be detected from the beginnings of the Nazi era.

In view of the importance of the year it is almost symbolical that the means by which Heydrich sought to implicate others beside himself were realised in January 1942 at the Gross Wannsee Conference. After a six-week deferment it took place on 20th January and delegates invited, besides RSHA officials, including Eichmann,

Adolf Eichmann at his trial in Israel

Herschel Grünspan's father gives evidence at Eichmann's trial

also numbered civilians from the Ministry of the Interior, the Foreign Ministry and other departments.

Despite the euphemistic language in which the matter was described to them there can be very little doubt his hearers perfectly understood Heydrich's meaning. Jews were to be used in labour gangs where a large part would 'fall out through natural diminution'. The remnant which survived – 'unquestionably the part with the strongest resistance' – would be given 'special treatment'. 'Special treatment' meant simply extermination. In this way some eleven million Jews – including those of Britain after conquest – were to be annihilated. Half-Jews were to be given the choice between death or sterilisation.

If Heydrich was afraid of an outburst of indignation from the assembled delegates his fears proved unfounded. Not a single voice was raised in protest. Dr Otto Thierack, Reich Minister of Justice even offered to hand over all Jews under his jurisdiction to the SD, and Eichmann, at his trial in Jerusalem in 1961, was able to recount how at that moment he sensed a deep contentment 'such as Pilate must have experienced, because I felt completely free of any guilt. Here at this Wannsee conference the most prominent people of the Reich were stating their views. The "popes" were giving their orders. Mine was to obey'.

The initial hurdle so successfully negotiated, the conference went into greater precision. In Eichmann's words: 'We went on to discuss the various possible ways of killing them.'

That this meeting can never have been anything but a ruse to incriminate others is shown by the fact that the matters discussed under the head of 'possible ways of killing' were suggestions already being energetically implemented: starvation, overwork, gassing, mass-shootings.

For Heydrich, however, the occasion was to prove something of a Belshazzar's Feast. He was never to witness the realisation of his plans. On 27th September 1942 he had been promoted to SS General and appointed Protector of Bohemia and Moravia. While visiting his domain he was assassinated by Czech partisans on 5th June 1942. For this crime a terrible price was to be exacted, including the total destruction of the village of Lidice and the massacre of most of its inhabitants.

After Heydrich's death Himmler did not appoint a successor for some six months, when he chose a former Austrian lawyer, SS Lieutenant General Ernst Kaltenbrunner, who was to prove in every respect a worthy successor. Indeed, from Himmler's position he was even superior, since he was a less ambitious man than Heydrich. During the interim period until Kaltenbrunner's appointment, Heydrich's duties fell on Eichmann, who on 6th March called a conference of his own, to discuss and seek answers to two problems. One was that of finding transport; the other was how sterilisation of Jews married to Gentiles and of their children was to be carried out. The second problem was never solved, despite hideous tortures inflicted on concentration camp 'guinea pigs'. Hitler did not want his hands tied if he decided to wipe out half-castes as well.

On 20th March 1942, three weeks after Eichmann's conference, 8,000 Jews of mixed marriages in Holland were offered sterilisation as an alternative to deportation. Sterilisations were actually carried out at the Dutch detention camp, Westbork, in some cases by SS doctors, but normally by personal physicians. This had been done without Eichmann's knowledge and his wrath on the heads

Horak's farm in Lidice

Ernst Kaltenbrunner

Oswald Pohl

of those responsible followed, but, in fact, it was being done under a private agreement between Himmler and the Higher SS and Police Leader for Holland, General Hans Rauter. As a result some 8,610 Dutch Jews were left at liberty as, in Rauter's words, they were now considered to be 'of no danger to Germany'. They did not even have to wear the Jewish badge, while those born impotent could get a certificate to this effect and were also exempt from the badge. This measure led to a new racket for the Gestapo who did a brisk business in the sale of 'sterilisation' certificates.

After Gross Wannsee Himmler pressed on with plans for making his concentration camps economically viable, appointing a former naval paymaster, Oswald Pohl, to head a new department of the SS to develop the slave-labour programme. He had already seen to it that such obvious opportunities for profit as the removal

of gold fillings from the mouths of the dead, and in some cases of the living, were not overlooked. Despite draconian sanctions intended to ensure that only the SS and no private person gained from such activities, under concentration camp conditions these were impossible to enforce and it is believed that hundreds of prisoners were killed for the gold in their mouths. One man, Kriminalkomissar Christian Wirth, an expert on extermination from the old euthanasia institutes, wandered the camps with an empty jam tin in which he collected gold fillings.

Even by 1942 there were still a number of renowned and distinguished Jewish figures – artists, musicians, scientists – living in Germany. Himmler was conscious that their sudden disappearance from the scene would have left too noticeable a gap. The disappearance of Jews with high war decorations, would also be embarrassing, notwithstanding Hitler's pronouncement that 'the swine got their decorations fraudulently anyway,' and for such men a special ghetto or reserve was earmarked. It was the fortress town of Theresienstadt in Bohemia, whose population had been evacuated by Heydrich as one of his first acts as Protector. The town had had a population of 7,000; it would soon have to accommodate 50,000 people.

Conversions and preparations were carried out and it was opened after a muted fanfare which included showing it off to representatives of the German and International Red Cross and to Danish officials. Himmler was even to boast, sanctimoniously, to a representative of the World Jewish Congress later: 'This type of camp was designed by me and my friend Heydrich and so we intended all camps to be.'

The mere existence of such a place, where despite overcrowding, there seemed to be a measure of security, would itself create a demand for places in it. This could easily be used by the Gestapo for a lucrative trade and thousands of Jews passed through its portals, believing they had bought their lives, only to go on to the death camps further east. At the same time crowding remained so intolerable that many even 'exempted' Jews were finally deported. Labour was compulsory and harsh. Rations were at bare subsistence level and some internees found they were hungrier than at the more notorious concentration camps. The most generous were those given to farm and mica workers: nine ounces of bread per day, with two ounces of potatoes and watery gruel. Sometimes as many as 130 people a day died from starvation alone.

A further lucrative racket for the SS lay in a 'home purchase scheme' thought up by Eichmann. Under this scheme, those to be sent to Theresienstadt had before departure to surrender all their assets. The excuse for thus stripping them was that these were to be used as security for house purchase and what remained of their money after this transaction was to be devoted to providing accommodation for those without means. Such a scheme was not without attraction since before emigration Jews had to declare any remaining assets which were then automatically confiscated by the government. In this way they appeared to be devoting them entirely to 'Jewish' causes (actually of course they were handing them over to the funds of the SS). On arrival at the ghetto they would discover what their

Camp money from Theresienstadt

Molotov

purchase amounted to: a bunk in a teeming hut – if they were lucky, for only sixty per cent of internees had even that luxury.

In Himmler's eyes, beside its other virtues, Theresienstadt was a useful means of countering atrocity propaganda, as whenever questions were raised about a famous Jew who had vanished he could be produced. And perhaps sensing that victory was no longer the inevitable reward of German arms both Himmler and Heydrich had been increasingly preoccupied with the possibility of their deeds being revealed. Stories of German massacres in Russia had been reaching the Soviet government through survivors and partisans and had drawn an angry denunciation from Molotov, the Russian Foreign Minister. A successful Russian offensive, even if finally checked, could lead to actual discoveries that would be more difficult to dismiss as propaganda than survivors' accounts.

Just before his departure for Prague in May 1942, Heydrich summoned Blobel of Babi Yar fame and assigned him the job of exhuming and utterly destroying the corpses in the mass-burial grounds. He was also to carry out the same functions at the extermination camps as they came into operation, advising their administration on methods of destroying the bones of the dead.

Blobel was to find himself fully occupied, for the massacres were still going on. On the last day of January, for example, eleven days after Gross Wannsee, Franz Stahlecker, the man who had instigated the pogroms in Lithuania, reported to Heydrich that 229,052 Jews had been executed in the Baltic States. In February and March it was the turn of Russia once more, where in Kharkov, the most easterly of the Ukrainian cities, lived some 81,000 Jews. Of these some 20,000 had been caught by the German occupation. In December they were moved into a 'ghetto', actually the disused huts of a tractor factory. From here they were taken in batches of a few hundred a time to be shot. Finally the huts, containing the bodies of many who had died of cold or hunger, were burned.

Thus the *Einsatzgruppen*, following so closely on the heels of the army that they sometimes became a threat to security, continued to reap fresh harvests. By September 1942 they had penetrated to their most easterly point: Kislovodsk, in the North Caucasus, where some 2,000 Jews from the town itself and several thousand others from Piatygorsk and Essentuki were shot. When the Red Army swept forward this was the first mass-burial place to be discovered. On 29th October 1942 the surviving Jews of Pinsk, totalling about 16,000 were liquidated.

But it was in Poland and particularly the eastern provinces of the General Government that the Final Solution was being most methodically applied. The Jews of Eastern Galicia had temporarily escaped the fate of others caught by the advancing Germans, because on 1st August 1941 the province was brought under Frank's administration as part of the General Government and thus was outside the operational area of the *Einsatzgruppen*. However, in December that year in a speech to his cabinet Frank announced that his domain 'must become free of Jews, the same as the Reich'. There is some evidence that he was preparing his own Final Solution, but this would not fit in with Himmler's plans at all, if only because the Reichsführer-SS and the head of the General Government rarely saw eye to eye, and in fact Himmler had already entrusted Odilo Globocnik with the task of carrying out 'phase four' of the operation to destroy all the Polish ghettoes and reserves. This was the planned reduction of the ghettoes by the expedient of liquidating those members of their population not essential in employment and thus not protected by work permits.

To this the code-name *Aktion Reinhard* was attached, fitly commemorating the memory of a man whose malign genius had been behind the Final Solution, the now dead Reinhard Heydrich. The consummation of his plans became possible as the mass-gassing installations at existing camps and at new extermination camps came into operation through the spring of 1942, though in fact at the first place selected the only means of execution were the gassing-vans used in Russia. These were diverted to Chelmno, a concentration camp centering round a derelict chateau ironically called 'The Palace', and intended for use as the Lodz ghetto. The gassing-vans continued to be used throughout the life of the camp, victims either being tricked into going into them or driven with whips, and altogether 152,000 Jews were murdered here.

In Lodz ghetto were some 30,000 people and a start in resettlement was made with Reich deportees and members of some of the smaller outlying communities. Between January and September 1942, 55,000 victims were moved from Lodz to Chelmno. Though the death-rate was high, the gassing-vans could only deal slowly with large numbers, and it was disease, hunger and overwork which accounted for most of the deaths. Indeed, the inhabitants of the ghetto were in such poor physical condition that those needed for forced labour had to be taken from other places.

Lodz, of course, was on the extremity of the Reich-incorporated territories and of the General Government, and one must remember that one purpose of this slaughter was to provide *Lebensraum*, under the terms of Himmler's brief as Commissar for the Strengthening of German Folkdom, for Germans brought back from abroad. By the end of 1941 a total of 497,000 including those from the Baltic States and Rumania had moved into an area formerly occupied by one and a half million Poles and Jews. By July 1942, 120,000 of them were still housed in camps. By August 1943, the number had increased to 546,000 and there were about 99,500 in camps and 22,000 near Lodz, all of them destitute. They were being clothed in garments taken from exterminated Jews.

Mid-March saw the opening of Belsec, the first permanent gassing camp. It had four gas-chambers each capable of holding 750 persons and it was charged with exhaust fumes from a diesel engine. In actual use the engine frequently failed to start and the victims could be left for hours locked in the chambers, their moaning audible outside. Nevertheless, it was here that 15,000 victims from Lublin, the 'Jewish reserve' were gassed. The rest, something like 11,000 went to Majdanek, where they survived at least until the gas-chambers there were completed in the Autumn.

During April it was Lwow ghetto which was resettled, when some

15,000 people were removed during the first month and others in May and June, though the movement was delayed because Belsec was overcrowded.

Other actions were at the same time taking place in the smaller ghettoes and by July 1942, some 250,000 Jews of the 1,600,000 in the General Government had been resettled.

And still the shooting continued. During that summer something like 7,000 murders a day were being committed. In the whole of Poland half a million Jews probably perished. In one of the biggest massacres, at Lida, 16,000 died. Göring was able to say to a conference: 'There are only a few Jews alive. Tens of thousands have been disposed of.' By the end of that year the figure of the slain of 250,000 in the General Government had leaped to 1,274,166.

It was from the scene of one of these

Above left: Lodz . *Below left:* Majdanek . *Below:* 'Resettlement'

blood-baths, at Dubno airfield in the Ukraine on 5th October, that one of the most complete accounts of what mass-execution meant to its victims comes to us. Hermann Gräbe, a German civil engineer, testified in an affidavit presented at the Nuremberg War Crimes trials, how he saw a mass of people lining up on one side of a large mound of earth. Among them was an old white-haired woman holding a child of about one, which she was crooning to; elsewhere a father was holding the hand of his ten-year-old son, stroking his head, while the boy fought back tears; a slim girl with black hair as she passed Gräbe, pointed to herself and said: 'Twenty-three years old'.

Gräbe, amazed he was not sent away, went round to the other side of the mound. There was a tremendous pit already holding perhaps a thousand bodies. Nearly all had blood running from their heads. Many still moved. Some were trying to show by raised hands that they

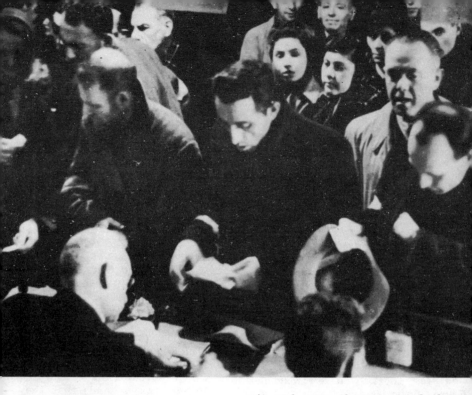

Registration for Treblinka

were still alive so that they could be put to death.

At one end of the pit an SS man sat, his feat dangling into it, a submachine gun across his knees, a cigarette drooping from his mouth. As the group of people Gräbe had seen on the far side were brought round he saw them climb into the pit, under the direction of the SS man. Then there was a series of shots. When he looked again some bodies still twitched. Others lay motionless.

He watched another group brought to the shooting place, including among them a paralysed woman, who had to be undressed and carried by others.

Next morning he returned to the spot. About thirty people had crawled from the pit and some had got some distance away. A few were still alive. Others had died. While he was there the SS party arrived. The living were ordered to carry the dead back to the pit and were then executed themselves.

Gräbe saw that all went meekly to their deaths, obeying orders intended to facilitate their own execution. None pleaded for life. None sought to escape. None resisted.

But resistance was to come.

The resettlement operations carried out under the Aktion Reinhard programme had still not accounted for the biggest ghetto in Poland – Warsaw. In this were some 380,000 inhabitants and in July, Globocnik, among others, felt that they had delayed overlong in tackling it. For one thing some 7,000 surviving Jews from Rowno ghetto, all of whom had been exempted because they had work-permits, had been killed that month. This was the nearest ghetto to Warsaw and hence the strictest precautions had been taken to see that what occurred did not become known there. These had largely been successful, but with every passing day the possibility of discovery would increase in Warsaw, and despair might cause its population to make a stand against resettlement.

For the delay, however, there had been good reasons. One was that there was a transport shortage caused by preparations for the Wehrmacht's summer offensive in Russia, as Hitler had promised that the eastern campaign would be decisively ended that year. Heydrich in fact had been prevented by the offensive preparations from sending any Jews to the Russian ghettoes from March onwards. But despite these demands Himmler was able to procure some trains from the State Railways. By July, when the offensive was just beginning there were a sufficient number to provide one a day to take Jews from Warsaw to Treblinka extermination camp from the day it opened. This camp, which went into action on the 23rd, was almost the last of the main death camps. The very last, Sobibor, was not opened until late October because of a mutiny led by a Pole in which about 150 Jews attempted a mass break-out. Most died in the minefield surrounding the camp, and only about thirty survived the war. It was followed almost a year later by a similar abortive revolt at Treblinka, again led by a Pole, this time a captain in the army. Jews broke into the armoury and took weapons, but the revolt failed and the rebels were massacred. Two months later, however, in November 1943, the whole camp was emptied, blown up and the mass graves cleared, and the area planted with pines. Notwithstanding these troubles, Sobibor and Treblinka, between them, managed to account for over a million lives of Jews from Russia, Czechoslovakia, Austria, Holland and France.

The sorting out process which began the Warsaw resettlement in 1942 and sent Treblinka its first and many subsequent victims, was carried out according to the established pattern, by picking on those with no work certificates, as well as on the old, the sick and children. The lists had to be provided by the ghetto's Jewish Council – thus the Jews here, as everywhere else, were made accomplices in their own killing.

America was not yet at war with Germany and for this reason Warsaw Jews who were US subjects were told to register and were sent to a prison – this should have been warning enough that something was about to happen, but there was at this time no resistance organisation in the ghetto. Thousands of Jews were known to be hiding within the walls, but conditions were such that many voluntarily joined the deportation columns for the sake of bread and marmalade travel-rations.

Although the German documents speak of 5,000 a day leaving Warsaw, the Jewish Council had been ordered to provide 6,000 a day and this could not go on indefinitely without involving certificate-holders. Now the Germans began what they had done in other places. They constantly changed the certificates, annulling earlier ones. Those not in possession of valid documents were rounded up and often the wives and children of certificate-holders would be dragged away while their husbands were at work.

By 15th August half the ghetto had gone and its actual area was reduced, the first of several such reductions. The next day a new work certificate was issued. It was limited to 30,000 workers and did not cover their dependents. Between 5th and 12th September a fresh round up was organised and over this period some 100,000 Jews, including Jewish Council employees and members of the *Ordnungsdienst*, the Jewish ghetto police, were resettled. Again the size of the ghetto was reduced. By 3rd October only about 30,000 Jews existed officially, though actually when those in hiding were included there were some 60,000 to 70,000 surviving.

Those Jews who remained, however, were largely unencumbered by de-

Above: A Jew is discovered in hiding in the Warsaw ghetto *Below:* A Polish resistance fighter is arrested

pendents and in this situation were prepared to accept the orders of the resistance group which now developed in the greatest secrecy. In the long run it was found that by breaking up families as they had the Germans had made a miscalculation.

The turn of the year found the Jewish Council, even with the numbers in the ghetto greatly diminished and those still there employed in armaments factories, trying to fulfil the quota of 5,000 a day. In January 1943 Himmler paid a surprise visit to Warsaw and was angered to discover far more people than he had expected. Resettlement, he ordered irritably, must be completed by 15th February.

Some German factory managers, trying to save their Jewish employees, sent false returns of their numbers and were even hiding them.

On 18th January, four days after Himmler's unscheduled visit, a column of deportees was marching to the transfer point, the Cauldron as it was called, when several of them drew guns and opened fire. Their arms were pistols of Italian manufacture and bought through the black market for something like £50 each. This pitiful fusillade was quickly and witheringly answered and the Jews withdrew to cover leaving their dead. For three days a hunt continued but even after field guns were brought up to demolish the north-eastern corner of the ghetto where some four resistance groups were holed up, they were not all destroyed and the Germans called off the action.

Himmler had now ordered that a concentration camp be built inside the ghetto and when completed all the buildings were to be flattened. Later both the Jews and the workshops in which they laboured would be transferred to Lublin.

Meanwhile, on 13th March Cracow ghetto was resettled. There were only

SS Major-General Jürgen Stroop interrogates a prisoner in the ghetto

Resistance fighters take to the sewers

some 14,000 Jews involved and the action was completed in two days, the inhabitants going to various labour and extermination camps.

The day the Cracow resettlement began, the Warsaw Jewish Council was ordered to produce 2,000 people for a transit camp at Trawniki. Neither the council nor its arm, the *Ordnungsdienst*, was able to carry out the orders. The resistance groups were in control and the council was caught in a cross-fire. If they disobeyed the Germans they went to Treblinka; if they obeyed they would be killed by the resistance. The Germans had to find their deportees for themselves.

On 17th April SS Major-General Jürgen Stroop arrived to take over the duties of Higher SS and Police Leader in Warsaw. Two days later he sent two armoured cars, three artillery pieces and a captured French tank into the ghetto. As a show of force their effect was nil and he had to break the ghetto into sectors to which units were assigned for 'pacification'.

Nor did he find cooperation among the German factory owners. Big shelters had been dug in the grounds of many of the factories, ostensibly against air raids. In these, large groups of Jews hid with the cognisance of their employers.

On 21st April Stroop was successful in getting over 5,200 Jews out of the army factory and deported. Later, he found that some still remained. They had disguised themselves in Germany army uniforms, stolen from the factory.

It was at this point that Stroop, under Himmler's orders, decided on the methodical destruction of the ghetto by fire and explosives. There had never been enough weapons for everyone, besides which a high pro-

The clearing of the ghetto

portion, the old and the sick, were in no condition to fight. Many of these groups, rather than surrender, preferred to die in the flames, though sufficient numbers were rounded up by 25th April for 25,000 to be sent to Treblinka over the ensuing days.

The battle was far from over, however. The resistance fighters took to the sewers and by this means made contacts with Polish partisans, who supplied weapons and sent fighters into the ghetto. In the end those hiding in the sewers were driven out by the use of smoke candles. They thought they were being gassed.

On 28th April a bunker in which some of the wealthiest and most important members of the ghetto had been living was captured. Hitherto, Stroop had avoided actually blowing up the bunkers for fear of damaging the factories and their tools. But now his policy began to change and several factories were dynamited. The bunker-dwellers, like others, chose to die where they were.

Some 1,100 troops were by this time engaged in the ghetto-clearance, not a large number in comparison with some partisan actions in which the Germans became involved, but humiliatingly disproportionate to the task. On 9th May, Stroop captured what he believed was the headquarters dugout and with it the deputy leader and the resistance committee. Even so resistance went on, though on 11th May he was told by a prisoner that the leaders had all committed suicide. Stroop accordingly decided to call off the action on the 16th.

Small numbers of prisoners fell into his hands, and though he had discovered that the remaining Jews expected to be able to come out of hiding and continue their lives when he withdrew, he stuck to his decision to wind up the battle. On 16th May, the day it officially ended, a synagogue and a Jewish cemetery were blown up. In the ghetto itself 7,000 Jews were said to have been killed and a large number had gone to Treblinka and other camps. But for months afterwards surviving resisters were being rooted out.

Himmler, when he heard of the action, commemorated by Stroop in a lavishly illustrated leather-bound report, ordered the whole ghetto area to be totally erased, all cellars and sewers to be filled in and the reclaimed land to be turned into a public garden. Work for this was to continue until the Warsaw Rising of the following year when the Red Army was not more than fifteen miles away.

Aktion Reinhard officially ended in October 1943, and that December Globocnik presented his 'profit and loss' account. It included not only lists of the numbers dead, but also of their possessions. Among them were, besides such items as clinical thermometers and alarm clocks, those gifts which people present to one another as marks of love or esteem: gold and silver propelling pencils, bits of jewellery, watches, cigarette cases, lighters. The value of these items amounted to 178,745,000 Reichmarks.

In the meantime Himmler was still involved in his business ventures. On 12th March 1943 the SS had founded their own company, Osti (East) Industries GmbH, with Oswald Pohl as chairman and Odilo Globocnik as managing director. Its purpose was to take over some of the factories being completed or already built in Lublin. Now that the exemptions of Jews working in the armaments industry had been revoked they would fall totally under the control of the SS. These included not only those in factories in Poland and elsewhere, but also those in the Reich itself whose deportation Göring had been forced to halt the previous year.

Every endeavour was at once made to move these Jews east and three deportation trains left Berlin taking munitions workers between January

and the end of February 1943, without attracting attention. But a fourth, on 27th February, was scheduled to transport many well-known Reich Jews and though the Wehrmacht factories were surrounded by units of the *Leibstandarte Adolf Hitler*, the picked bodyguard formations, the round up largely failed. The Jews had been warned. Four days later another effort was made and this time was interrupted by a tremendous RAF raid on the capital. Then there was a demonstration from an angry crowd after an attempt to drag off people from a home for the aged. The whole action had to be stopped and it is worth noting that the proportion of Reich Jews, as a whole, sent to the death camps was well below that from elsewhere. From a 1933 census figure of 499,682 Jews in pre-war Germany 123,000 are estimated as killed. Some 180,000 Jews were deported by May 1943 of which 100,000 were sent to Theresienstadt, where about 60,000 died. There were always large numbers in hiding; in 1943 probably about 40,000.

Nevertheless, Globocnik was able to boast that with the Jews from all sources, there were 45,000 slaves employed by Osti. At the same time he was complaining that they were failing to get orders. Himmler hated to hear of failure and Globocnik was already falling out of favour after some dubious exchange dealings, and he was shortly to be relieved and posted to his home town, Trieste. He is said to have committed suicide in June 1945.

In June 1943, he had a further proposal, for which in the end no credit was to redound to him. This was to move Jews from Litzmannstadt, near Lodz, to Lublin and to close the Litzmannstadt camp. In Litzmannstadt there were still people working in exempted industries and at once these were inundated with orders – to save them from 'resettlement'. Himmler had had enough of Globoc-

Warschau, den 16. Mai 1943

Az.: I ab - St/Gr. - 1607 Tgb.Nr. 652/43 geh.

Betr.:Ghetto-Großaktion.

An den
Höheren ƻ– und Polizeiführer Ost
ƻ–Obergruppenführer und Genral d. Polizei Krüger
o.V.i.A.
K r a k a u

Verlauf der Großaktion am 16.5.43, Beginn 10.00 Uhr:

Es wurden 180 Juden, Banditen und Untermenschen vernichtet. Das ehemalige jüdische Wohnviertel Warschau besteht nicht mehr. Mit der Sprengung der Warschauer Synagoge wurde die Großaktion um 20.15 Uhr beendet.

Die für die errichteten Sperrgebiete weiter zu treffenden Maßnahmen sind dem Kommandeur des Pol.-Batl. III/23 nach eingehender Einweisung übertragen.

Gesamtzahl der erfaßten und nachweislich vernichteten Juden beträgt insgesamt 56 065.

Keine eigenen Verluste.

Schlußbericht lege ich am 18.5.43 bei der ƻ– und Polizeiführertagung vor.

Der ƻ– und Polizeiführer
im Distrikt Warschau

gez. Stroop
ƻ–Brigadeführer
u. Generalmajor d. Polizei

F.d.R.

ƻ–Sturmbannführer.

nik's maladroitness and cupidity. In early September, Oswald Pohl took over his functions as managing director of the ten Osti camps. But Himmler was tired of these as well. On 3rd November five of them were closed down. Without any of the Osti executives being told, a massive selection was made and in the most intensive single massacre of the

Stroop's report confirms the destruction of the ghetto

Final Solution a total of 16,000 Jews were machine gunned in pits in a matter of hours, then cremated. The figure has even been put as high as 40,000. During the mass-burning the whole town of Lublin was covered with dust.

Auschwitz

The spring of 1942 had seen another landmark in the completion of the Final Solution. This was the coming into operation of the huge gas-chambers at Auschwitz, each one capable of taking 2,000 victims at a time. This camp more than any other has come to be synonymous with extermination so that to say someone had 'gone to Auschwitz' automatically implied his death. This was true even among the other concentration camps, for Jewish Internees were moved from the German camps to Auschwitz during the October of 1943 and only a small minority of these were expected to be capable of work.

Himmler himself preferred Auschwitz to any of his other camps. He told Rudolf Höss, when he commissioned him to enlarge the camp to include extermination facilities, that it was 'favourably placed as regards technical communications and . . . it will be easy to close off and camouflage the area.' The camouflage of which he spoke was an I G Farben synthetic rubber factory, employing camp labour, though this was sited at Monowitz, some distance away. Auschwitz was actually three quite separate camps, of which Monowitz was one. The concentration camp proper was simply called Auschwitz or Auschwitz I. and the extermination camp, about three kilometres from it, in the Birkenwald, was called Auschwitz II or Auschwitz-Birkenau.

For this some 20,000 acres of countryside had been cleared of habitation. Only SS men or civilian employees with special passes were allowed into the area. All the equipment of mass-death was hidden deep in the woods and in the words of Höss 'could nowhere be detected by the eye'. This was not strictly true.

It could be seen from the railway and passengers crowded to the windows to look at the high chimneys, knowing, apparently, perfectly well what they were for.

Auschwitz I and Auschwitz-Birkenau were, individually, the biggest camps in Germany. Thus, as commandant of this complex Höss could feel himself a person of some consequence. Höss was the forty-two year old son of a Baden-Baden shopkeeper, destined to become a priest. He broke with the church at the age of twenty-two and joined the NSDAP. In 1923 he had received a life sentence for his part in killing a schoolmaster said to have denounced an early Nazi to the occupying French.

In prison he met Martin Bormann, who was to head Hitler's Party Chancellery. The Nazi takeover in 1933 found him still in prison, but in 1934 he became a blockleader in Dachau Concentration Camp, a position accorded to trusted prisoners. In 1936 he became a second lieutenant in the *Totenkopf Verbände*, the concentration camp guard units. Thus, this convict and concentration camp inmate crossed the seemingly impassable divide between guarded and guard and, having made the leap, rose to the rank of lieutenant colonel of the SS. A photograph taken of him at his trial in Warsaw shows a man with sensitive and anxious eyes, in many ways the expression of a conscientious priest, who despite outward piety is prey to doubts. 'A personality,' Dr G M Gilbert, the Nuremberg psychiatrist said, 'not entirely of this world.' Höss acknowledges that though he carried out the Führer Order on exterminations he suffered grave misgivings.

The area under his command, the concentration camp group called

Auschwitz, lay just outside the General Government in an area of southern Poland which had been absorbed into Silesia. Thus, this the biggest of the death camps was geographically within the Reich as defined after the fall of Poland.

Efforts to disguise the function of Auschwitz-Birkenau were not limited to external 'camouflage'. As at other camps (Treblinka, for example, had its mock railway station), pains had been taken to allay the suspicions of new arrivals. Some of the gas-chambers were underground, others on a level with the crematorium. All were fitted inside with shower-douches. The ground over the gas-chambers had been laid out as lawn and here the Birkenau gipsy-orchestra serenaded the condemned with selections from Franz Lehar and Strauss. The grass expanses were broken only by the tops of the tubular ventilators, down which the

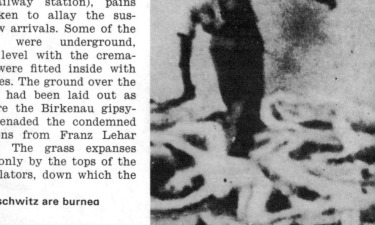

Victims of Auschwitz are burned

Women and children arrive at Auschwitz

Zyklon B crystals were thrown. Both the grass and the ventilators were quite common in German military practice and would not have aroused suspicions, though later the function of the bunkers was fully known to all, including those about to enter them.

Even the buildings of the crematoria were not outwardly unpleasant, though the size of the chimneys might have seemed disproportionate to their purpose.

On a normal day this tranquil aspect would hardly be disturbed, except for the smoke coming from those very chimneys, for everything, including the lilting strains of the *tzigane* orchestra was designed for the smooth, uninterrupted destruction of men, women and children.

The picture built up in the postwar world of Auschwitz is of a continuous

Martin Bormann

flow of transports bringing fodder for the gas-chambers. In fact, there were killing seasons, which corresponded with the round-ups being carried out through Eichmann's Department IVA4b of RSHA. During the 'season' which lasted from four to six weeks, two or three trains a day each brought an average of 2,000 people – enough for a single filling of the chambers. Before each consignment left for Auschwitz a teletype would be sent from 116, Kurfurstenstrasse giving the numbers to be expected and incorporating the formula 'to be treated according to the directives for special treatment'. On arrival the train would be shunted into the Birkenau siding. As a security precaution not only was the locomotive detached and the railway personnel ordered out of the area, but also the guards who had accompanied the train. Camp guards now took over. Such devices largely failed as the railwaymen managed to get photographs of Auschwitz and Treblinka 'bath houses' and sold them, knowing

perfectly well what they were. Some even found their way back to the Warsaw ghetto.

For the passengers the next stage was the process of selection by SS doctors. Over the whole two and half years these were made they were always carried out on the spot and for the same reasons: anyone liable to become an encumbrance – young children, mothers with babies, pregnant women, the sick and the aged, were automatically moved from the column of the living to the column of the moribund, often with no more than a cursory wave of a walking-stick.

Those temporarily reprieved would then be marched away to the work-area of Birkenau or to Auschwitz main camp.

Those chosen for death, who were sometimes joined by others brought from the camps themselves, were then led to a group of buildings in which they were told to strip for showering or 'delousing', then they went down the ramp into the gas-chamber, if it was below ground, or along a corridor in the open which had barbed wire fences along either side, if it was above ground. Once inside the great iron doors clanged echoingly shut and they waited for the water to flow from the douches above their heads.

Above, on the grass, the mushroom caps of the ventilators would be unscrewed and on the order, 'Give 'em their feed', the cyanide crystals were dropped down the shafts. These terminated inside the chamber in perforated metal pillars. After a time the effects of the gas would be felt within and there would be a rush to get out, people hurling themselves at the door, scratching at it, tearing at one another. Death took between five and fifteen minutes, depending on the weather.

The only way that those waiting outside could tell that this had

Vents on the roof of a gas chamber

happened was because inside all became silent. The last screams died away. Then the exhausters would be switched on and the Special Commando, itself made up of Jews, who would end their own lives in the gas-chambers, dressed in gas-masks and boots reopened the chamber. The dead, now a solid mass, would be separated with ropes and hooks so that the looting of teeth, hair and spectacles could be carried out. Then the corpses would be conveyed to the crematorium furnaces by lift or by rail wagon, according to which chambers had been used. The bodies disposed of, the bones (on Blobel's advice) would be ground to powder in a bone-mill.

This was the process to which the name *Sonderbehandlung* – Special Treatment – was given.

It was, however, only the capacity of Auschwitz which helped to make it the chosen place for the international application of the Final Solution. What was happening there was larger in scale, but in no other way different from all the other extermination centres. Its sheer size has imbedded it in the folk-memory of Europe.

So in Greece, as in the existentialist poetry of France, the name occurs in the 'new music' to be sung to *bouzouki* accompaniment. For here, of an estimated 67,000 Jews before the war, just over 10,000 survived. From Salonika alone, where there was the biggest of the Greek Jewish communities something like 45,000 were taken.

In Yugoslavia, not all of which was under German occupation, some 55,000 Jews probably perished. The city of Belgrade was declared Jew-free in July 1941. In Croatia, which had been created an independent state, some 20,000 Jews took refuge with the Italians, who had interests in the area. The Germans began diplomatic efforts to get them back, but

The camp orchestra

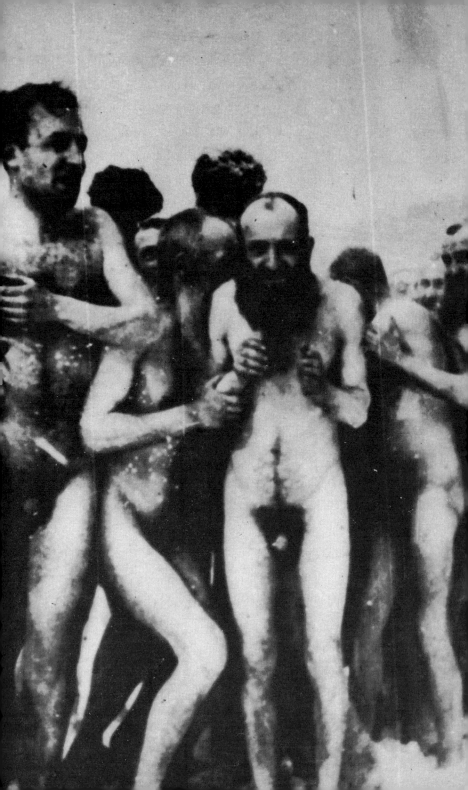

Before the shower

their hosts introduced all kinds of delays and confusions so that, in the end the Germans had to be content with the 21,000 they had managed to lay their hands on.

Hitler's dictate had been quite specific: every Jew in Europe was to be annihilated. So not only in the east, but also in the west the name Auschwitz resonates like a terrifying shriek out of a dark forest.

Foremost among the nations of the west was, of course, France and in 1942 there was still concern at 116 Kurfurstenstrasse at the lack of enthusiasm shown there for the Final Solution. The RSHA were inclined to blame themselves for not having insisted in May 1940 on the kind of deal which had worked so admirably in Russia where their *Einstazgruppen* were independent of the army and solved the Jewish problem *ad hoc*. It was difficult in France and Belgium to introduce even the star of David and this was not done until June 1942 and then in the face of opposition.

To try to get things going on the right footing in October 1941 a bungled attempt had been made to destroy two synagogues so that it would appear as if the French wanted to be rid of their Jews. No one was deceived and the attempt was traced back to a French Gestapo informer. This nearly became an international incident.

When, however, there was a series of attacks on German soldiers this was used to better effect; 1,000 Jews and 500 Communists were ordered to be deported for 'forced labour' in the east.

In the west the Germans had not established ghettoes. They persuaded the governments of the countries under their dominion to open local 'internment camps'. These were useful in several ways, one of which was in easing the consciences of those collaborationists who at the same time

Hair (Above) and artificial limbs (Below) removed from corpses

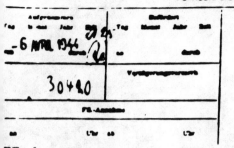

Der Befehlshaber der Sicherheitspolizei und des SD
im Bereich des Militärbefehlshabers in Frankreich
Fernschreibstelle

-6 APRIL 1944

30420

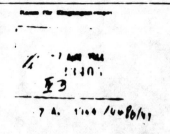

7 A. 1144 /4486/41

LYON NR. 5269 6. 4. 44 2010 UHR -- FI -

AN DEN BDS - ABT. L. ROEM 4 B - PARIS -

BETR: JUEDISCHES KINDERHEIM IN IZIEU-AIN

VORG: OHNE

IN DEN HEUTIGEN MORGENSTUNDEN WURDE DAS JUEDISCHE

KINDERHEIM '' COLONIE ENFANT '' IN IZIEU-AIN AUSGEHOBEN

INSGESAMT WURDEN 41 KINDER IM ALTER VON 3 BIS 13 JAHREN

FESTGENOMMEN. FERNER GELANG DIE FESTNAHME DES GESAMTEN

JUEDISCHEN PERSONALS · BESTEHEND AUS 10 KOEPFEN.

DAVON 5 FRAUEN BARGELD ODER SONSTIGE VERMOEGENSWERTE

KONNTEN NICHT SICHERGESTELLT WERDEN --

DER ABTRANSPORT NACH DRANCY ERFOLGT AM 7.4.44 --

---

did not wholly support the excesses of Nazi antisemitism. As long as the interned Jews were on national soil, they could feel that everything was all right and even Jews themselves, free and interned, shared this delusion. Because of it the Germans were successful, until their true plans became known, in having large numbers rounded up and incarcerated in the camps, whence they could be quietly removed for extermination conveniently.

In Occupied France there was such a camp at Drancy and from here between April and June five trains left for Auschwitz, each carrying about 5,000 people.

German report on the seizure of a Jewish children's home at Izieu-Ain and the dispersal of its inmates and staff

Eichmann had had his eyes on bigger hauls than this, however, and on 16th July a great round-up into which much planning had gone, took place. In this it was hoped that at least 22,000 stateless Jews in Paris would be brought in. Actually the operation netted just under 13,000 including some 4,000 children. Of this 13,000, 6,000 were sent straight to Drancy, the rest, including all the children, spent five days in a sports stadium, the Vélodrome d'Hiver. The adults

King Christian of Denmark

Departure to Drancy

were then sent to Auschwitz and the children to Drancy. From here they were consigned to Auschwitz in due time with French gendarmes, to their immortal shame, helping to drag the screaming little ones to the trains of death. In November, Belgian railwaymen going through box-cars returned empty from the east, found the bodies of twenty-five children, aged between two and four.

These were Jews in the world's most civilised city under Hitler's Third Reich.

By the end of the summer 25,000 Jews had been deported from Occupied France, though not one had left Vichy Territory. Efforts to persuade the Pétain government, through its foreign minister Laval, to revoke naturalisations which made Jews French citizens proved, in general, useless. Eichmann could fume as much as he liked as the trains came back unfilled or were cancelled for lack of freight.

Even after the occupation of the whole of France in November 1942 Jews were still able to find sanctuary in the Italian zone in the south. For though Mussolini had brought in anti-Jewish measures of his own as early as 1938 these gained so little public support that they could never be enforced.

In the country of France's neighbour, Belgium, the internment camp was Caserne Dossin in Malines. From 4th August 1942 a train service intended to take Jews to Auschwitz was running, but attempts to round up Jews were proving difficult with the Belgians showing an active sympathy towards them. Saws with which their prisoners cut their way out were smuggled into trains; railwaymen managed to leave the doors of some trucks open; and once a train was caught in an ambush they had organised and from which 150 Jews escaped. Nevertheless, some 25,000 Jews were deported.

Across the border in Holland in the second half of July 1942 5,742 Jews were taken via a camp at Westbork to Auschwitz. However, as in Belgium, deportation was proving uphill work. Many Jews began to go into hiding with Dutch Gentile families (best known among these is the teenage diarist, Anne Frank, hidden in a warehouse). Unable to find their quota of Jews elsewhere, the Germans turned upon the helpless, on old peoples' homes, orphanages, mental institutions. The only requirement was that the transport trains did not go back empty. This demand was met even when, as in one case, mentally-sick children were packed so tight in a cattle-truck that attendants could not reach them. It took them four days to get to Auschwitz whence neither children nor attendants were ever seen again. But these, too, were Jews in Hitler's Third Reich.

Attempts were also made to impose the Final Solution on Occupied Scandinavia. In Norway some 725 Jews were rounded up by German police and Quisling militia in November 1942. All but twenty-six were deported and a further 158 followed in March 1943. Only thirteen survived the war. A larger number, however, some 900, were slipped across the border into neutral Sweden by the Norwegian underground.

In Denmark, where the Germans were in occupation of a neutral country, efforts to use diplomatic as well as other pressures to impose the Final Solution failed almost totally. There were two prime reasons: one was King Christian's brave stand – he said that if the Star of David was introduced, for example, he and his court would be the first to wear it, and he made a show of attending Jewish feasts at Copenhagen synagogues. The second reason for failure was the fact that, as in Norway, the Danes managed to slip many Jews out of the country.

A gas generator at Struthof concentration camp

Eichmann's efforts were not limited to the countries Germany held in subjection. Through Department Deutschland III of Ribbentrop's Foreign Ministry pressure was brought upon Germany's allies in its war with Russia and even upon neutrals like Spain and Portugal – unsuccessfully in both cases. At Gross Wannsee it had been agreed that the Slovak, Croatian, Bulgarian and Hungarian governments were all to be approached and told that the Germans were willing to rid them of their Jews. In Hungary, a country allied with Germany against Russia, an estimated 180,000 Jews perished out of the large numbers deported to eastern Europe. Even in late 1944 and early 1945 some 30,000 to 40,000 Jews from Hungary, including women and children and the old, were deported, some to help in the building of the South East Wall intended to keep the Russians out of Vienna. Only a small proportion ever returned. Negotiations to gather in still more were continuing to the moment of Hungary's surrender to the Russians and Eichmann, who was in the city, escaped from Budapest only at the last moment.

In Rumania, another of Germany's allies, with a population of 692,000 Jews, as many as 220,000 may have died. Bulgarian Jews were rather more fortunate. Out of a 1939 Jewish population of 50,000, 46,500 had survived till the end of the war. Attempts to impose the Final Solution came up against every sort of obstacle, not least public demonstrations when Jews were deported. The Rabbi of Sofia was even supposed to have been hidden in the home of the Orthodox Metropolitan, Stefan.

Diplomatic representations were made through Ribbentrop to Slovakia, the satellite produced by the dismemberment of Czechoslovakia after the Munich agreement. Some 17,000 male Jews were deported to Auschwitz in March 1942 – allegedly for labour, as well as 10,000 others later, of which 7,000 were children. So totally were the authorities and Jews themselves taken in by the story that they were to be used for labour that in due course the families of the deported men applied to follow them. By the end of June 52,000 people had left but at the end of the war only 284 survivors were found. After making repeated requests to visit the work camps, the Slovak government, which was predominantly Roman Catholic, were warned through the Papal Nuncio what was happening to deportees. The movements were then brought to an end but the Germans had to be bought off. Wisliceny, Eichmann's representative, was promised 55,000 dollars if he went to Berlin to get the transportations stopped. Just to make sure the money was forthcoming another 3,000 Jews were sneaked out of the country.

In Italy, offers to take care of the country's Jews were made, but gained no response and it was not until 1943, when the Germans took over after the armistice that they had a free hand. Then something approaching 10,000 were deported and even Rome, the eternal city, was not spared. Under the nose of the Vatican, which raised not a finger to save them, 615 were rounded up for Auschwitz.

And as these hundreds of thousands from all over Europe travelled to the gas-chambers of Treblinka, Sobibor, Majdanek, Belsec, Chelmno and most of all Auschwitz-Birkenau, it is no wonder that there were times when the victims entering the famous 2,000-person gas-chamber had to do so with their arms raised above their heads, so that more could be packed in; so that children had to be thrown in to die on the heads of adults; and so that those for whom there was no room had to be shot in the neck outside. Then everything would be done at frenzied speed, the Special Commando working under the blows of rubber truncheons and whips.

At such times the output of corpses would be too great for the crematoria.

It was found that the best method of disposing of them was by burning them in pits into which petrol had been poured.

These were the occasions when the order on which Höss prided himself, the systematic disposal of humans, broke down. Even in conditions more nearly normal the process was one which the man with troubled eyes could not bear to watch. He generally left it to his camp security chief, Captain Fritzsch. Sometimes, however, he was compelled to be present in person. Then: 'I had to watch coldly while mothers with laughing or crying children went into the gas-chambers. . . . My pity was so great that I longed to vanish from the scene: yet I might not show the slightest trace of emotion.'

During his examination at Nuremberg he was asked about his pity: 'How was it possible to carry out these actions in spite of this?'

'In view of the doubts which I had, the only one and decisive argument was the strict order and the reason

'Most of you know what it means when a hundred corpses are lying side by side . . . '

given for it by the Reichsführer Himmler'.

If perhaps sympathy fails when we compare the lot of Höss with that of those at his mercy, then we can console ourselves with the thought that Himmler was always deeply compassionate towards Höss and his kind in the terrible task he had asked them to undertake. So he speaks to a meeting of Higher SS and Police Leaders in 1943: 'Most of you know what it means when a hundred corpses are lying side by side or five hundred or a thousand. To have stuck it out and at the same time – apart from exceptions caused by human weakness – to have remained decent men . . . This is a page of glory in our history which has never been written and is never to be written.'

But with the establishment of the extermination camps, with Eichmann's Europe-wide railway system

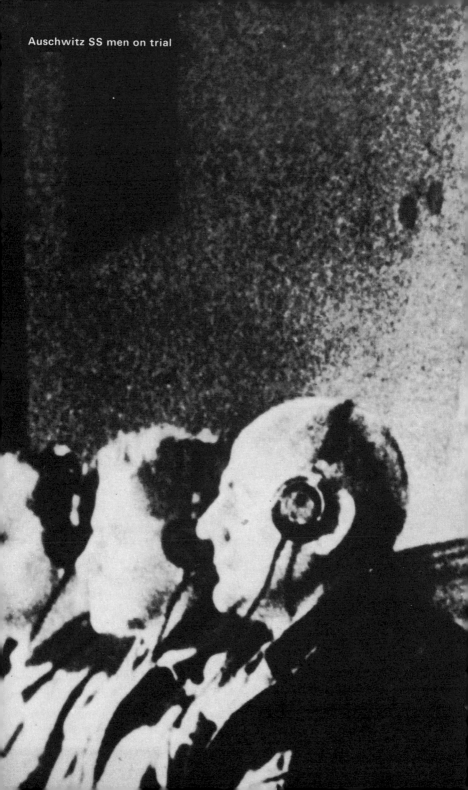

Auschwitz SS men on trial

of death running to schedule, the story is still not finished. In some eight major Russian and Polish ghettoes liquidation was being carried out.

The first to be tackled was Lwow where 'resettlement' began on 21st June and ended six days later. The Lwow Jews did not give in without a fight and here the weapons were more terrible than the pistols of the Warsaw resistors. Lice infected with spotted typhus had been bred in the ghetto and some 120 of the SS men carrying out the action were affected with the disease.

It did little to prolong the lives of Lwow Jews. At a shooting site out of town, the 'Sand Hill', save for a few survivors ultimately found by the Red Army, nearly the whole ghetto population of 20,000 met their deaths.

From Sosnowiece, the next ghetto to be cleared, some 25,000 – virtually all the Jews there – were sent to Auschwitz. All but 500 were gassed immediately. The action lasted a week.

At Bialystok, where the next action began on 21st August, progress was slower. The extermination camps were choked, besides which many of the Jews were employed in textile factories in the town regarded as essential. When they were finally rounded up an attempt at a break-out was made. It failed with heavy casualties among the Jews. Those who survived – some 25,000 – were all sent to Treblinka.

Of the Polish ghettoes only Lodz with a population of 85,000, was left. Of the communities in Russia and the Baltic States the first to meet its fate was Minsk on 14th September. Here had lived the 8,500 survivors of the *Einsatzgruppe* massacre, their numbers having been whittled down over the succeeding months by gas-van killings. The remainder, which included many Reich Jews, were killed in the same way.

In Vilna, Lithuania, were about 20,000 of which some had been tricked

into going to the Ponary death pits already used by being told they were to be resettled at Kovno ghetto, supposedly better off. An attempt at resistance as the resettlement programme got under way produced only a fracas at the railway station and most went to the camps. When the Russians overran the town they found some 600 Jews hiding in the sewers.

In Riga resistance never went beyond the talking stage and the town's 15,000 Jews were reduced to 4,000. About half went to labour camps. The rest were put on trains which shunted round the railway system until about a quarter had died of cold and starvation. The remainder went to Auschwitz.

Kovno ghetto contained about 20,000 people of which some 7,000 were from Germany and Lithuania. When this number had been reduced to a few thousand the president of the Jewish

Council begged that they might be allowed to wait for liberation by the Russians. This the Gestapo at first seemed disposed to allow, but at the last moment all were sent to Germany.

It was now the turn of the reprieved Lodz where mass-evacuation was started in the August of 1944. By the middle of the month, the population, starving and terrified, had been reduced from 85,000 to 61,000. During the succeeding weeks they too, were distributed among the camps.

On 17th December 1942, the United Nations declaration that those who practised extermination on the Jews were to be punished had been read to the British House of Commons. Members stood in silence. The gesture, if touching was totally empty, for almost a year before to the day a steamer left the Rumanian port of Constanza, with 769 Jewish refugees,

The massacre at Minsk

among them seventy children, bound for Haifa in Palestine. They were without immigration permits. The vessel broke down off Instanbul. The Turkish authorities refused to allow its passengers to land until the British gave permission for them to proceed at once to Palestine. This was categorically refused. After ten weeks the ship was towed out to sea by Turkish tugs where it broke up and sank. Two people reached shore, the rest were drowned.

After well over a year of massive genocide, details of which were perfectly well known to the government, there was no sign that the callous policy laid down by the 1939 British White Paper of restricting Jewish entry to Palestine was in any way changed.

Out of the chaos

he possibility of German defeat which had loomed in 1942 had, by the autumn of 1944, come to look more and more inevitable. Hopes for an Allied victory increased after the D-Day landings of 6th June had installed Allied armies on the European continent.

The extermination camps had now been functioning for two years, causing the deaths of untold numbers. While, at the same time the Red Army had been advancing steadily, pushing the Germans out of their most recent gains, out of Russia altogether and backwards through Poland and the countries of Hitler's allies, Hungary, Rumania, Bulgaria.

On 24th July they were in Lublin – where there were no longer any Jews – and the Allied press carried its first stories of the concentration camps and exterminations, for war correspondents were shown the small gas-chambers (Majdanek, the Lublin camp, was never a mass-extermination centre in the full sense), the crematoria, cans of Zyklon B and samples of human bones.

What remained of Jewish populations in the line of their advance was not, so far as lay in Hitler's power, suffered to fall into Russian hands. They were driven out of the reach of liberation into Germany. Where this could be not done they were

Auschwitz inmates liberated by the Russians

The 'hospital' at Buchenwald

summarily executed. The movements westward had begun as early as the summer when 27,000 Jews were evacuated in July from nine camps in Radom and Cracow and nearly 4,000 from the camp in the former Warsaw ghetto, as well as from other camps. On the march hundreds were machine gunned and those who survived were sent straight to Auschwitz.

When this was not possible the migrants were simply packed into the German concentration camps. There were now 500,000 people in these – a number which of course the selections and 'natural diminution' were, and very effectively, reducing. It was thought by the mid-summer of 1944, nevertheless, that twice this number could be brought into the camps, but only about 100,000 more Jews were admitted, mainly because the Germans were fearful of epidemics if greater numbers were crowded in.

In the minds of the captives there was by now a clear understanding of what their fate would be. If they did not die of hunger, overwork or disease, or fall out on some route march to be shot by their guards, they would finally be exterminated *en masse*. Auschwitz was, after all, working at its greatest pressure at this time and it was in May (admittedly before D-Day had changed the look of the war) that Himmler had spoken with unusual candour about the Jewish question. The Jews, he told a meeting of Nazi officials at Posen, were to be rooted out, killed – he actually brought himself to use the word – men, women and children. 'We were forced to come to the grim decision that this people must be made to disappear from the face of the earth,' he told them, as if he were announcing new measures against fowl pest.

Washing facilities at Dachau, intended for up to 800 people

Yet things were not as they seemed.

Himmler had had some profound thoughts about his own future in a defeated Germany subject to the United Nations. In particular, he thought of his hostages. Already an exchange camp had been opened at Bergen-Belsen concentration camp and in May, the month of his speech, Eichman had had a meeting with Joel Brand, of the Budapest Zionist Relief Committee, during which a deal to barter the lives of 700,000 Hungarian Jews for 10,000 heavy lorries for the German war machine was discussed. These were to be supplied by the Allies through Salonika, but the whole thing came to nothing after the story had broken in the Allied press.

Then, in July, another proposal was put forward, this time by another Budapest Zionist, Dr Reszoe Kastner. This was for 100,000 Jewish lives in an outright deal for five million Swiss francs. Himmler looked at the terms and came up with his own proposition: 30,000 physically fit Jews for six million US dollars. They were not to be handed over, but to be kept 'on ice' at the Austrian labour camp, Strasshof. Only 1,800,000 dollars was raised and for this price 9,000 Jews were 'put on ice'.

Negotiations again broke down altogether when Kastner was told that Himmler was determined not to let a single Jew leave Europe, though on the question of the Bergen-Belsen Jews, among whom was a group of 1,684 Budapest Jews, there might be room for manoeuvre. Talks reopened, this time in Switzerland and as a display of good faith on the German side some 318 of this group of Budapest Jews were pushed across the border at Basel. The Germans now formulated a proposal to stop not only the deportations, but also the gassings in exchange for deliveries

of *matériel*. But this the Jewish negotiator was in no position to offer. Instead he returned with an offer of 15,000,000 Swiss francs as the price for calling off deportations from Czechoslovakia and Hungary, to be followed by the release to Switzerland of the remaining Bergen-Belsen Jews.

The money for this purpose (in all 20,000,000 Swiss francs) was collected in the US through charities and the transaction might have been successfully completed, but that Cordell Hull, the US Foreign Secretary, would only allow five million of the sum to be transferred to Switzerland. Edward Stettinius, jr, who succeeded Hull very shortly afterwards, cancelled even the transfer of the five million and not until 6th February did Himmler receive it, through the president of Switzerland Jean-Marie Musi. A total of 2,684 Jews were then moved to Switzerland. During the winter an actual meeting between Himmler and Musi was arranged. This time in exchange for money, instead of equipment and medical supplies, which Himmler had originally demanded, 1,200 Jews were to be sent by train to Switzerland every fortnight. One of the terms of the deal was that a new propaganda climate was to be created in the rest of Europe in which Germany should cease to be regarded as the murderer of Jewry.

The plan reached the ears of an enraged and outraged Hitler, who told Himmler to issue an order that all camps were to be destroyed and their inmates killed if they were in danger of being overrun.

Some good had, however, already come from the inconclusive negotiations and particularly from Himmler's anxiety to 'change his image'. In October of 1944 gas-chamber selections at Auschwitz stopped. In September, in fact, a mission from the International Red Cross had actually been allowed into the camp, though only for an interview with Baer, the commandant who had succeeded

German civilians are expected to observe exhumed bodies of victims of a route march across Czechoslovakia

Höss. But British POWs working at the synthetic rubber factory, who were interviewed, drew the mission's attention to the gassings. This information was second-hand and when they tried to get it first hand from internees they refused to talk. Following the mission's visit, however, there was an improvement in camp conditions.

Then, in November, an order went out from Himmler for the crematoria to be dismantled. Auschwitz was at the end of its two-and-a-half year life of murder. Höss had boasted of killing 2,500,000 Jews. But the most reliable figure, horrific enough in all conscience, is 840,000. They came from Belgium, Croatia, France, Germany, Czechoslovakia, Greece, Holland, Hungary, Italy, Luxembourg, Norway, Poland, the Baltic and Slovakia, the biggest total, 380,000, coming from Hungary, and about 180,000 others from Poland and the Baltic. Of this the great majority, between 550,000 and 600,000 were probably gassed on arrival, 'selected' from the transports as they came into Birkenau siding. But there were in addition to the total a large number from the camp itself, probably numbering hundreds of thousands, who were gassed, being termed 'no longer fit for work'.

The Jews of the Special Commando, which handled the corpses at Auschwitz after gassing, knew perfectly well what fate awaited them with Himmler's new order, and attempted an abortive revolt. Late in November they were taken out into the Birkenwald and shot.

As the Russian advance approached the camp inmates began to be distributed through the other camps in Germany. These first movements were comparatively orderly, a number of women at Birkenau going to Bergen-Belsen, which Josef Kramer,

Josef Kramer and Irma Grese, in command at Bergen-Belsen

commandant at Birkenau in its heyday as the principal extermination centre, had been sent to organise.

Later, with 64,000 people still in the camp and Russian guns within earshot, evacuation became chaotic. Thousands travelled only in their striped prison uniform in open rail wagons and in winter weather. Others travelled on foot. They were distributed to Dachau, Dora, Mauthausen, Ravensbrück, and Sachsenhausen, with the largest number of all, 13,886, going to Buchenwald.

When the Russians arrived at Auschwitz on 26th January they found only 2,819 invalids in the three camps most of whom they were able to nurse back to health.

There were now, in the encircled Reich, some 700,000 concentration camp inmates. The lives of all of them were deteriorating daily and in proportion to the deterioration of conditions within Germany. This was not in the least helped by the fact that not only Himmler, but also other SS leaders were planning, in secret, ways of saving their own skins with the Allies. Often these covert activities came into conflict with each other or with those of some super-idealist of the Final Solution, like Eichmann, who would do his utmost to sabotage his colleagues' schemes.

Himmler himself was currently engaged in a fresh round of negotiations aimed at circumventing the order to destroy the camps and their populations. On 12th March he agreed to hand over the camps intact and to stop all executions of Jews. On 19th April Dr Norbert Masur, director of the Swedish section of the World Jewish Congress, arrived in Berlin, met and had talks with the archenemy of the Jews. Himmler, still terrified that Hitler might discover what he had done, could not be tied down to specifics, but some sort of agreement was worked out with the assistance of Kersten, Himmler's masseur, who had done much already

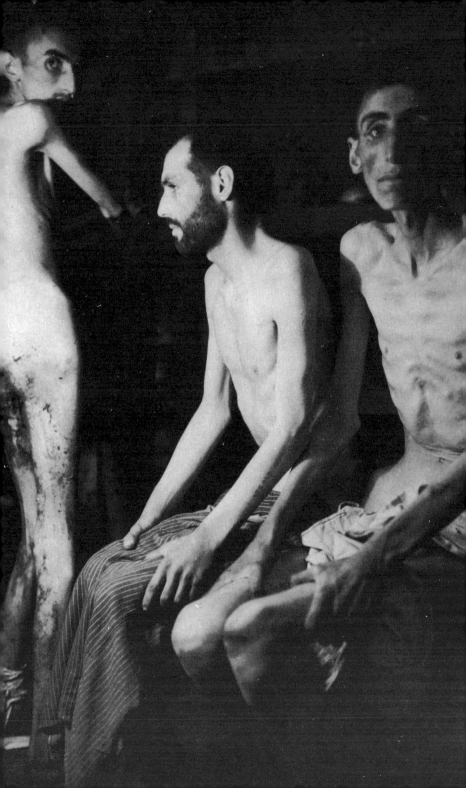

to advance these life-saving negotiations.

Yet still a chess-game with human lives went on. The Swiss Red Cross representatives were trying vainly to get into the camps, to talk openly with internees and form some estimate of the sort of aid that was going to be necessary. The Swedish Red Cross representative, Count Folke Bernardotte, managed to penetrate Neuengamme, near Hamburg, but the best the Swiss had been able to do was to talk to an Oranienburg internee in the presence of his keepers and of leading SS officers.

The first concentration camp discovery had, of course, been Russian and this the Germans tried to slough off as Communist propaganda, an answer to their own Katyn wood discoveries of the year before. Now, however, another Allied force was nearing Buchenwald. These were the Americans and on 3rd April a mass-evacuation began. More than half the 48,000 people of the main camp were sent to south Germany by train. A few days later 4,500 Jews in one of the satellite camps followed; 1,500 were dead on arrival at Dachau. All this was despite Himmler's promise that the camp would be handed over intact.

At about the same time British troops closed in on Bergen-Belsen. The discoveries there have become famous. In Camp I 40,000 people were found living among 13,000 unburied corpses. Their condition was such that some 13,000 of those living died after liberation. The place was riddled with typhus; probably as many as 40,000 people, mainly Jews from Hungary and Poland, had succumbed to the disease.

All the Allies have since been criticised and in many ways justifiably, for making such enormous and speedy propaganda capital out of their concentration camp discoveries. By what they did they ensured that

Starvation

Count Folke Bernadotte

the Germans would see to it that no more were handed over unevacuated if it could possibly be helped. And the matter was now taken out of Himmler's hands, Hitler ordered that every camp inmate who could walk must be driven from the camps.

When the point was reached that no further evacuation was possible they were to be slaughtered. This almost came to be realised in the case of Dachau where there was a plan to put those from the surrounding camps in it and then bomb it from the air. In fact, events moved too swiftly and it was handed over to the Americans with only part of its population evacuated on 24th April.

At Theresienstadt, where the Red Cross representative had been promised by Eichmann there would not be a single deportation, it was learned on 12th April that all camp records had been destroyed. This made it look as if a massacre was envisaged. The camp was now suffocatingly overcrowded with evacuees from four other camps squeezed in with its normal population. However, by

Above: German red cross official identifies evidence at Katyn. *Below:* Eisenhower, Bradley, Patton and other US generals watch a reconstruction of concentration camp torture. *Left:* Women's quarters at Bergen-Belsen

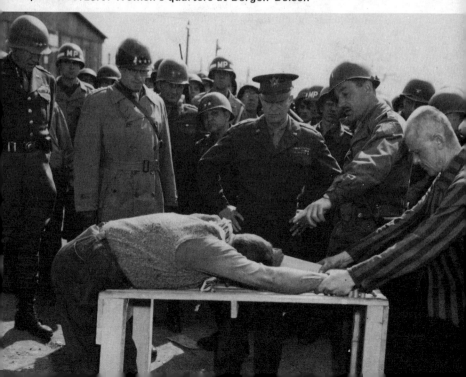

prompt measures by the Red Cross their flag was flown from the camp and all within were saved from the perils of execution or evacuation.

All over Germany the Red Cross delegates were now fighting to save what was left of the concentration camp populations. At Mauthausen, swelled like all the others by people evacuated from other camps, they were successful in stopping a plan to put the prisoners in an underground aircraft factory and blow them up. On 8th May the camp was handed over to Patton's troops.

Even now and with the end days away the evacuations did not stop. At Oranienburg the prisoners were moved almost within sight of the Russians and with the Swedish Red Cross officials powerless to help. All they could do was follow the column, bringing up food and taking the sick back to the Allied lines. At the same time from Sachsenhausen and Ravensbrück similar columns of starving, worn out, hopeless men and women were being marched towards the last pockets of Nazi resistance. An order had, however, been given which broke established practice on these occasions: stragglers were not to be shot. They were picked up in Red Cross lorries.

As their saviours bent down to lift them up, from sheer habit the prisoners begged not be to shot.

The progress continued to the last days of April – to the very days when Hitler was writing his will and binding his successors to the continuance of the policies he had followed.

It was only a few days later that the war in Europe ended.

Hitler was dead. Dead, too, were Heydrich and Himmler. Kaltenbrunner was soon to be brought to trial and subsequently hanged. Eichmann had vanished. So also, for

the time being, had Höss. Many others were to be unearthed in the years that followed; some have never been discovered.

But also numbered among the dead were untold hosts of the Jews of Europe. In 1939, according to figures computed by the American Jewish yearbook for 1946-47, the Jewish populations of Germany, its allies, satellites and subject nations, was 9,282,500. By 1946 it was 3,169,000, a drop of nearly two-thirds. The two countries which suffered the greatest loss were, as might be expected, Austria and Germany. The German 1939 Jewish population of 240,000 had fallen to one-twentieth of that number; the Austrian population of 60,000 to one-twelfth. By no means all of this can, of course, be attributed to the Final Solution. As far as Germany and Austria were concerned much of it is accountable to the massive exodus after the war. It is not necessary that we should look in detail at the figures, nation by nation, they are, in any case, speculative, and even the total death-roll is put variously at six million and about four and a quarter millions, with four and a half millions now most commonly accepted as the most accurate.

But even for those who survived the holocaust, unconditional surrender brought no solution to the vast problems, physical and psychological, that the Nazi régime and the Final Solution had created.

It was to be almost two decades before the 'Displaced Persons' camps emptied while an oblivious world, the same oblivious world which had allowed the Final Solution to come to fruition, went about its business. And it is a mere platitude to say that, veiled behind human apathy, what had taken place was the most frightful crime ever committed in the bloody history of man. Its enormity, and the complexity which sprang from that enormity were such that they defy coherent or complete telling. It was, in every respect, the acting out

of a psychosis on a national scale. And it is perhaps because of this that, highly documentated as it is – thanks largely to its perpetrators' devotion to order and procedure – it is still surrounded by mysteries which arise from the intrigues and the need for secrecy among the men who, for all the excuses of their racial theories, knew they were committing a crime. Already there exist libraries of books upon it and none tells all there is to be told; many treat only a single facet or incident, the story of one camp or one massacre.

It is yet another platitude to say that for all its enormity it was utterly and wholly useless. It gained for the Nazis not the slightest advantage.

For all the fulminating about Zionis plots, the rehashed lies from 'Th Protocols of the Elders of Zion', th supposed financial conspiracies (international Jewry, in twelve year of persecution with millions of word of Jewish documents passing throug their hands, they extracted very littl useful propaganda material fror them. The Jews were not the al powerful force of Hitler's imagina tion; neither in Britain nor in Americ were they able to muster the suppor which could have saved at least large percentage of them, while suc evidence as the Nazis found tende only to show Jews as men and wome who thought themselves no le German than their persecutors. I

Hungarian Jews released from camps return to their homeland

he synagogues the majority prayed
iot for the success of apocryphal
conspiracies but for their country
and its rulers, as in British synagogues today they pray for the Queen
and the nation, using the forms of
the Book of Common Prayer. Such
was their patriotism that old established families of German Jews refused
to leave the country and awaited
'resettlement' with their bags packed,
in their homes.

Far from gaining by it, the Germans
contributed to their own downfall
with the Final Solution. It ultimately
urned the world against them, of
course, but it led them to a suicidal
waste of talent, skill and labour.
There was, too, the vast misapplica-

tion of limited technical resources,
such as the tying up of a transport
system already under pressure from
Allied air raids. Because of this,
vital supplies often failed to reach
the front. There was the blocking of
roads when thousands of prisoners
were evacuated, all at a time when
the nation was fighting for its survival. Eichmann would laugh glee-
fully if the last train to leave a city
before its fall was one bringing condemned humans to the death camps.

The adherence to the schedules
of the Final Solution must have
increased communication difficulties

157

for the fighting forces far more effectively than any resistance movement could have done. And it did greater damage than this to the German cause. It has been cogently argued that had the Germans conducted themselves differently during the Russian campaign, had Hitler not issued his notorious orders which made it 'a war without chivalry', the outcome might have been quite different. The Baltic States were fretting under the Stalinist yoke. Thousands had been deported to try to break their nationalist and independent spirit. There were other such groups in Russia itself, which could, and in some cases did, throw themselves in on the German side, for it is sometimes forgotten that modern Russia is still an empire of independent nations gathered under a central government by despotic and brutal tsars. If Hitler wanted to destroy Bolshevism this could well have been his means of doing it. His barbarities made it possible for Stalin to demand of his people that they fight a 'patriotic war'. And in this the *Einsatzgruppen* played no inconsiderable role, for whatever a population may feel about a minority within its borders, the sight of its destruction at the hands of an occupier, even one he is prepared to regard as a liberator, is not one in which the principle of 'mine enemy's enemy is my friend' is likely to apply. Particularly when, as happened with the *Einsatzgruppen* so little care was taken to see they were executing the right people. German administrators, like Wilhelm Kube, were led to protest that not only Jews, but ordinary Gentile inhabitants with no Communist connexions were being plundered and shot. And even had they been more scrupulous they would have done well to remember that such displays of naked violence do nothing to build confidence among the 'liberated'.

Belsen today. German youths on an outing

There is always the uncomfortable feeling that they too may go the same way.

The Final Solution was not just one crime of an immensity previously unimaginable and with one single victim multiplied infinitely. It was three vast crimes of which that committed upon the Jews was only the first. The second was that which could bring men, otherwise no more wicked than their fellows, to so abandon the innate decencies that they could lend themselves to it as accomplices. It is merely futile self-deception to try to believe it was all the fault of the system. Men pre-dated the system; but for them it could not have been inaugurated. If there was a system at fault it was one older than the Nazis. It was the ancient human system of complacency, apathy, moral cowardice, of taking the line of least resistance.

The third great crime was one perpetrated against the totality of the human race. Before the second decade of this century the best that men could do in portraying Hell was to be found in Dante's 'Inferno' or in the paintings of Bosch or Durer. We now have some excellent real-life analogies: Flanders, Hiroshima and the Final Solution. And of the three the Final Solution is the one most closely corresponding to the classical image of Hell.

Furthermore, what men had done, what they had been once, they could do and be again. The first crime always makes the subsequent ones more probable. One has only to think of Europe before 1914 to see what three decades and three visions of Hell have done to what was once a belief in the ultimate goodwill even of enemies. The Final Solution has left us permanently suspicious and fearful, for the racial theories which could lead to the Jew being the chosen victim of one persecution could lead to another group being selected for the next.

Bibliography

Hitler's Europe edited by Arnold and Veronica Toynbee (OUP, London)
Scroll of Agony by Chaim Kaplan (Hamish Hamilton, London)
Heinrich Himmler by Roger Manvell and Heinrich Fraenkel (Heinemann, London)
Gestapo: Instrument of Tyranny by Edward Crankshaw (Putnam, London)
The Final Solution by Gerald Reitlinger (Vallentine, Mitchell, London)
Anatomie des SS-Staates by Helmut Krausnick and Martin Borszat
(Walter-Verlag A.G., West Germany). Published in English, in abridged form,
as '*Anatomy of the SS State*' by Paladin, London.
Hitler: A Study in Tyranny by Alan Bullock (Odhams, London. Harper-Row, USA)
God's First Love by Friedrich Heer (Weidenfeld and Nicholson, London)